OMAHA BEACH

TUESDAY 6TH JUNE 1944

Christophe Prime

OMAHA BEACH

TUESDAY 6TH JUNE 1944

OREP
EDITIONS

CONTENTS

LCVP off Omaha Beach.

INTRODUCTION

Omaha Beach has become an essential heritage site for anyone with an interest in Second World War history. On the 6th of June 1944, a bloody yet decisive battle took place over these 5 miles of sand located around Colleville, Saint-Laurent and Vierville-sur-Mer.

The Normandy American Cemetery and Memorial, the sanctuary of Pointe du Hoc and the many museums and military vestiges proffer the site with striking emotional power. The French and American governments, together with the people of Normandy, strive to uphold the memory of this battle and of the American soldiers who fell so that Europe could be liberated from the Nazi yoke.

The battle on Omaha has become the symbol of the abiding bond between the United States and France, as was the commitment demonstrated by Major General Gilbert du Motier de Lafayette who set off to offer his support to the American insurgents in their battle against the British Crown.

The GIs who landed on Omaha on the morning of the 6th of June were caught off guard by the remaining German defences, which their high command believed to have annihilated. Although the outcome of the operation was a victory for the US Army, the bloodshed it suffered and the extreme violence of the combat it waged over several hours left a lasting mark on soldiers from both camps, also raising a number of questions. It has taken historians 70 years to clarify the last remaining grey zones.

Reconstructing such an event requires that we linger sufficiently on details. Men who found themselves a few yards from each other may well have a totally different outlook on events. Witness accounts and photographs are essential in order to fully absorb the story, and to share the fear, the suffering and the courage of these men. Objects and documents provided by veterans or found on the battlefield are also fantastic conveyors of memory and emotion.

The lines of beach obstacles in this picture are similar to those installed on Omaha Beach. © Bundesarchiv

CHAPTER 1

THE BEACH OF THE GOLDEN SANDS

DRÔLE DE GUERRE

Cast iron road sign found in Colleville-sur-Mer.
© Big Red One Museum

In September 1939, as elsewhere throughout France, the life of those who lived near the Beach of the Golden Sands was shattered by the declaration of war against Germany. Five million men were mobilised, forced to leave their homes to take up their postings. These soldiers resolutely awaited the enemy, yet no major offensive action was engaged. The armies remained, arms at the ready, for 8 months. The term "Phoney War", or "Drôle de Geurre" as employed by the writer Roland Dorgelès, later to be generally adopted, resumed the strangeness of these early months of the war.

On the home front, the war disrupted daily habits and generated difficulties and fear. The absence of men meant that women needed to provide for their families' needs and to manage farms or businesses alone. They lived with the constant fear of losing a father, a husband or a son. Mutual aid was essential. In April, the empty seafront villas were requisitioned to house refugees. The Piprel casino-hotel on Vierville beach was used to accommodate Parisian scholars and their teachers. The army requisitioned horses, before establishing food rations. A patriotic militia watched over the coast to identify any potential intrusion by enemy agents.

The seafront before the war.
© VD Collection

... TO THE STRANGE DEFEAT

On the 10th of May 1940, Hitler launched the *Fall Gelb plan* (the Manstein Plan). The *Wehrmacht* simultaneously attacked the Netherlands, Belgium and Luxembourg. On the 13th, Guderian's *Panzers* crossed the Meuse in the Sedan region and thrust towards northern France, catching the French command off guard. The French campaign was sealed in just 4 weeks. The Normans saw the arrival of columns of refugees from Belgium and the north and east of France. Some of them stayed and rented the vacant residences on the Golden Sands. The Belgian queen mother and her suite were among those who spent a few days in the area. The villagers strove to relieve those who had lost all by offering them food and lodgings; however, the capacity to accommodate very quickly reached saturation point.

The French Army Corps tried in vain to establish a demarcation line via Caen, Vire and Avranches to protect Cherbourg and to enable ships to cast off for England. The 154th Brigade of the 51st Highland Infantry Division landed in Cherbourg on the 13th of June to defend the peninsula. However, the tanks belonging to *Generalfeldmarschall* Erwin Rommel's *7. Panzer-Division* succeeded in bypassing the French defences. They gradually captured Caen, Bayeux then Saint-Lô before heading for Cherbourg. The French and British troops valiantly resisted. Offshore from the Bay of Veys, the old battleship *Courbet* and the *Roule* minesweeper

A column of *Panzer 38* (t) tanks belonging to the *7. PZD* at a standstill on a road somewhere in Normandy. General Erwin Rommel is observing the surrounding area. © Bundesarchiv

bombarded the roadways taken by the motorised enemy columns. Their action hindered the German progression sufficiently to enable British troops from the Norman Force to embark for England.

On the 17th of June, Marshal Pétain invited the French troops to cease combat and, the following day, requested that an armistice be signed with Germany. The *Panzers* from the "Phantom" division reached the southern outskirts of Cherbourg. The defenders of the Fortress of Cherbourg ceased all combat on the 19th of June. Rommel received Vice Admiral Le Bigot's surrender.

France's brutal and unexpected defeat resulted in an armistice that paved the way to 4 years of military occupation.

French civilians packed inside a cart on their way through a village ravaged by combat. © VD Collection

A German armoured column on a French road in June 1940. © DR

"LIVING LIKE GOD IN FRANCE"

For over 4 years, France's inhabitants lived with German soldiers who imposed upon them all sorts of interdicts and harassments. Forced separation was exacerbated by the anguish associated with increasing violence, bombardments and, in towns in particular, shortage of supplies. Requisitions and dearth worsened over the months. Nevertheless, the presence of farms and the possibility of gathering shellfish enabled the daily rations to be improved somewhat.

During the summer of 1940, Normandy was an operational zone within which a large number of German units were stationed awaiting the launch of the invasion of England (Operation *Seelöwe*). In 1941, the opening of new fronts led to the departure of combat divisions. Reserve units, together with police units, were deployed along the French coast to ensure its continued surveillance. As from the spring of 1942, divisions that were sorely afflicted by combat in the East were sent to western France to rest and to complete the ranks. New units, still under military instruction, were also regularly sent there.

Around a hundred soldiers occupied the sector stretching from Vierville to Saint-Laurent. The Château de Than, which was the property of the Poivre family, at the time resident in Paris, was requisitioned to serve as the *Kommandantur*. The *Wehrmacht* and the staff from the *Luftwaffe* in turn requisitioned hotels, the town hall and several villas in Vierville. Officers and their subalterns were accommodated in the most luxurious properties. The "Rinascente" villa,

August 1940, soldiers from the *12. Schutzen-Brigade* (*4. Panzer-division*) at rest in Vierville-sur-Mer.
© VD Collection

Newspaper dated 2nd October 1941 found in Cotentin. This publication was issued to the troops in charge of watching over the Channel coast. © VD Collection

Prohibition poster published by *Feldkommandantur 722* in Saint-Lô. © Omaha Beach Memorial Museum

Letter box reserved for use by German soldiers, found in the Colleville sector.
© Omaha Beach Memorial Museum

OPERATION AQUATINT

On the night of the 12th to the 13th of September 1942, around midnight, a British MTB 344 launch crossed the English Channel with 11 commandos on board. Carried off course by the current, the boat stopped 200 metres from the beach in front of the valley that leads to Saint-Laurent-sur-Mer, located around 4 kilometres from its original target, the village of Sainte-Honorine-des-Pertes. The detachment from the Small Scale Raiding Force commanded by Major March-Phillipps reached the beach aboard a canvas Goatley boat. They had been sent to collect information on enemy positions and to bring back prisoners. Yet, shortly after landing, the commandos noticed German soldiers on patrol. The patrol dog that was with them spotted the intruders and sounded the alert. An intense fusillade ensued. Automatic rifle fire and grenades launched from the WN 69 forced the commandos to swim back to the launch. The vessel became the enemy target and retreated from the shoreline after recovering two commando members. The skirmish had lasted thirty minutes. Major March-Phillipps, Sergeant Alan Williams and Private Richard Lehniger were killed. Two wounded men lay on the beach. Of the 4 men who managed to escape, only Captain Graham Hayes managed to evade the German patrols.

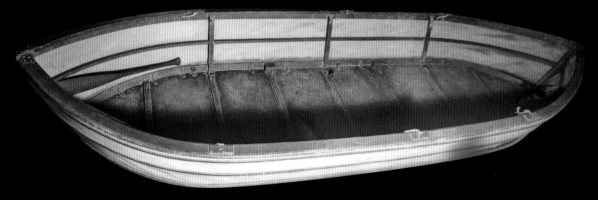

During Operation Aquatint, British commandos reached the beach aboard a Goatley boat like this one.
© Overlord Museum

located above the casino hotel was used by the *Kriegsmarine* as a radio relay station for submarines. The casino hotel was later to accommodate military detachments on leave and convalescent troops.

The Château de Than which housed the Kommandantur. © DR

In October 1941, the coastal band was declared out of bounds over a width of around 15 to 20 kilometres. Only permanent residents were allowed to travel and to live within this zone. Those who lived outside the area were only permitted to enter it if they presented a temporary *Ausweiss* delivered by the German authorities. As work on fortifications and mining progressed, access to the beaches was finally forbidden to the entire population.

THE *ATLANTIKWALL*

When the United States entered the war alongside Great Britain and the Soviet Union following the Japanese attack on Pearl Harbor, Adolf Hitler adopted a resolutely defensive strategy in the West. On the 23rd of March 1942, directive N°40 prefigured the creation of the Atlantic Wall (*Atlantikwall*). This formidable wall of concrete and steel running from the North Cape to the Spanish border was supposed to hold back any attempted Anglo-American landing. A few months later, the construction programme was extended to cover the Mediterranean coast, following the Allied landings in North Africa.

With the exception of ports, the western European coastline was, as yet, poorly protected. Faced with the multiplication of British commando raids, Hitler ordered for the creation of coastal

Sample of concrete cast on the 8th of May 1944 for an element of *WN 61*. © Big Red One Museum

defences to be accelerated. The construction of fortifications was entrusted to the Todt Organisation. The project was titanic: over 3,000 miles to cover, 15,000 concrete structures to build and 3,000 artillery pieces to protect.

> "To hold back with certainty all attempted landings, even those made by more important enemy forces with the smallest number of permanent troops."
>
> OKW Directive dated 14th December 1941.

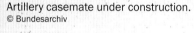

Artillery casemate under construction.
© Bundesarchiv

Joseph Goebbels, Reich Minister of Propaganda

The Germans initially concentrated their efforts on submarine bases, ports and the Nord-Pas-de-Calais region due to its proximity with England. Strongpoints held by small garrisons, a few poorly protected coastal batteries and radar stations ensured the defence of the other French coasts.

On the Beach of the Golden Sands, the majority of the villas that line the seafront were destroyed to clear firing angles and to deprive assailants of potential shelter. Access to the beach was permanently forbidden to inhabitants, as was shellfish gathering.

OT armband and insignia.
© Mémorial de Caen

Member of the OT talking to a French worker.
© Bundesarchiv

THE TODT ORGANISATION (OT)

After having undertaken major work during the period prior to the war [*Autobahn* (motorway); *Westwall* (Siegfried Line)] in Germany, the Todt Organisation built submarine bases and coastal artillery batteries in the Pas-de-Calais area before being entrusted, in 1943, with the mission of building the *Atlantikwall* then, launch bases for V1 and V2 rockets. The OT served as an intermediate between the *Wehrmacht* and the building and public works industry. It planned construction sites, negotiated markets with companies and managed site supplies both in terms of material and manpower.

The Todt Organisation mobilised over 200 German companies, together with French firms within the framework of requisitions or economic collaboration to build fortifications. It employed troops specialised in fortifications (*Festungspioniere*), civil engineering companies and RAD units – the Reich's work department. Manpower, prisoners-of-war and companies in occupied nations were requisitioned, willingly or forcefully. In June 1944, the Todt Organisation used some 300,000 men across its constructions sites. From this total, around a third were French and the other two thirds were of other origins, including Spain, Russia, Poland, Czechoslovakia and even Italy, all of them considered as forced labourers.

TIME WAS SHORT

Adolf Hitler's dreams of grandeur faded during the year 1943, with his armies' retreat on the Eastern Front against the Red Army, but also in the Mediterranean. After being chased out of Tunisia, Italy and southern France were in turn under threat. The opening of a new front on Europe's western coasts became increasingly probable.

Hitler appointed *Generalfeldmarschall* Erwin Rommel as general inspector of the North Sea and Atlantic coasts in November, before placing him in charge of the *Heeresgruppe B*. The Führer and the German high command continued to believe that the Allies would choose to land in Pas-de-Calais; however an assault in a different sector, the Bay of Seine in particular, remained an eventuality for which the *Wehrmacht* needed to prepare.

During his inspections, Rommel noted that several coastal sectors had been neglected, in Normandy and Brittany in particular. Beyond major ports, coastal defence amounted in fact to very little: rudimentary combat positions in insufficient numbers to offer mutual support, poorly camouflaged and ill-protected artillery pieces. Such was Rommel's conclusion at the end of his first inspection round. This sharp tactician was well aware of his adversaries' firing power and the superiority of their aviation. The Field Marshal knew that, in the case of a landing operation, the Allies would vigorously bombard the German defences which, if they remained as they were, would be irremediably annihilated. Reinforcing their protection was therefore of vital importance. He knew that it would be extremely difficult to throw the enemy back to sea, if he succeeded in setting foot on the Continent.

Lacking in armoured vehicles and planes, and with only modest infantry divisions at his disposal, Rommel had fortification work accelerated, placing priority on defending the Breton and Norman beaches. The fortifications needed to be reinforced without delay and reserve units placed as close as possible to the coast to ensure immediate intervention if necessary. Rommel

"The Wall was a monstrous bluff, less so for the enemy who knew what to expect thanks to its agents and other sources of information than for the German people. Hitler never saw the Atlantic Wall, not even part of it..."

Extract from *Generalfeldmarschall* Gerd von Rundstedt's interrogation in 1945

37mm antitank gun installed in a rudimentary position on the hillside.
© VD Collection

considered the beach to be the principal front and the enemy needed to be wiped out there within the first 24 hours. Any later would be too late.

These defences needed to be strengthened, casemates needed to be built for artillery pieces, bunkers for the infantry, trenches needed to be hollowed out, new minefields created and barbed wire networks installed. In the case of an attack, the positions needed to be able to defend themselves from all directions, and to offer each other mutual cover. Lines of obstacles needed to be installed along the foreshore to prevent barges from being grounded.

Aerial photograph taken where the Vierville valley opens out onto the plain on the 30th of June 1943. Several villas have been razed to the ground, including the casino. © NARA

The shoreline was transformed in just a few months. Around 500,000 obstacles were installed and 5 million mines of all sorts were buried on the beaches and inland. Strongpoints and coastal artillery batteries were endowed with bunkers and casemates. Minefields, ditches and antitank walls blocked the beach exits. To counter any possible parachute drops or glider landings, thousands of 2 to 3 metre-long wooden stakes, nicknamed Rommel's asparagus, were installed in the fields located inland, whilst lowland areas, marshes and valleys were deliberately flooded. A second line of defence was drawn further inland.

"Goth, they will come to your territory! This bay must be reinforced without delay to counter any attempted Allied landing, for Europe's fate will be decided here..."

Generalfeldmarschall Erwin Rommel.

1 Colonel Ernst Goth: commander of the *GR 916* belonging to the *352. Infanterie Division.*

German soldiers placing wooden beams on the foreshore. The water jet on this picture was used to hollow out the sand in order to work faster. These obstacles were surmounted by antitank mines covered with tar. © Bundesarchiv

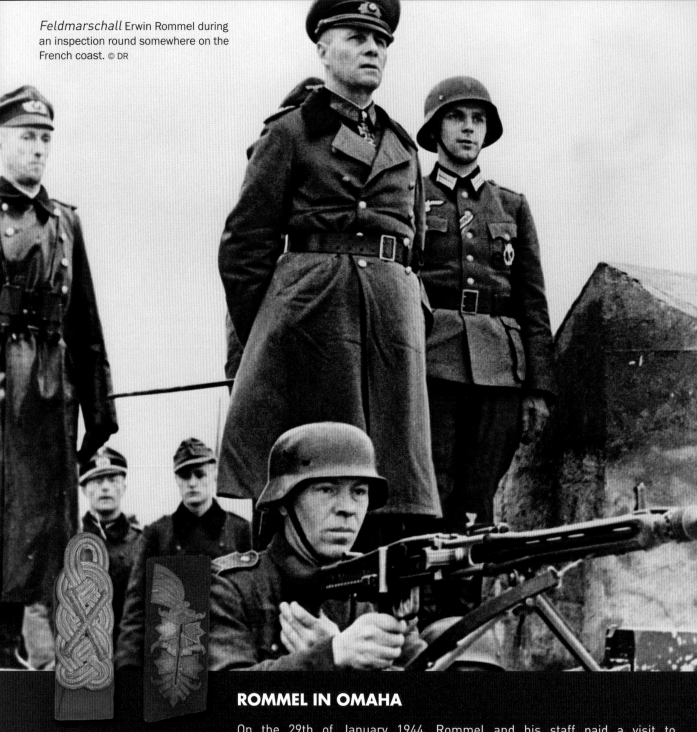

Feldmarschall Erwin Rommel during an inspection round somewhere on the French coast. © DR

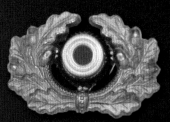

Epaulette, hat and collar badge worn by Rommel in 1944, donated by his son Manfred Rommel in 1997. © Mémorial de Caen

ROMMEL IN OMAHA

On the 29th of January 1944, Rommel and his staff paid a visit to *Widerstandnest* 62 ("resistance nest" *WN 62*). He was immediately struck by the resemblance with the Bay of Salerno, where the Allies had landed in September 1943 with no artillery preparation and leaving on-site defences intact. The American troops were stopped in their tracks, suffering small losses. The beach lined with escarpments prevented any inland manoeuvre, proving to be the ideal terrain for defenders and a potentially deadly trap for the adversary. Yet, to ensure that it fulfilled this aim, positions absolutely needed to be reinforced and soldiers trained in and accustomed to combat. On the 10th and 11th of May 1944, Rommel once more inspected the Normandy coast, defended by the *LXXXIV. Armeekorps*. He noted the progress that had been made in just a few months, even if very much remained to be done.

THE 716. INFANTERIE DIVISION

Insignia of the 716. *Infanterie Division.*

Officially created on the 2nd of May 1941 in the German region of Biefeld, the *716. Infanterie Division* was sent to the Lessay sector the following summer. After a few weeks of instruction in Soissons, then in Belgium, the unit returned to Normandy in March 1942, entrusted with the defence of the coast from the Orne estuary to the Vire estuary, hence replacing the *323. Infanterie Division* which had been sent to the Eastern Front. *Generalleutnant* Otto Matterstock was in command of the division until the 3rd of April 1942, when he was replaced by General Wilhelm Richter. The *716. ID* was a static unit (*Bodenständige Division*) exclusively in charge of coastal defence. This essentially horse-drawn division (1,500 horses), benefited from limited mobility. In December 1943, its numbers were reduced to a skeleton. The division comprised 9,343 men, whereas the theoretical manning of an infantry division was 17,000 men.

The division comprised two infantry regiments, each with three battalions, reinforced by three volunteer battalions from the East (*Osttruppen*), an artillery regiment and support units.

In 1944, the division was left with only 7,771 men, most of whom were convalescent wounded soldiers, very young recruits or older men taken from the rear guard. Although these soldiers were perfectly familiar with the sector, many of them had no combat experience. As for the majority of static divisions, each regiment had been deprived of one battalion in order to make up for the losses sustained in the East. Richter had at his disposal a grand total of 2 regiments and 3 battalions to protect the entire Calvados coast. Yet supplies of automatic firearms and artillery enabled the unit to maintain an appreciable, although insufficient,

Insignia worn by Ukrainian soldiers from the *439.Osttrupen- Bataillon* commanded by Hauptmann Hans Becker and assigned to the *726. IR.*

firing power. Three *Osttruppen* battalions were brought in to compensate. These auxiliary troops were essentially former Soviet prisoners-of-war who had chosen to don the German uniform to escape certain death. These troops, who lacked genuine motivation, were deemed of little reliability in combat.

The *GR. 736* (Grenadier Regiment) was deployed in the Dives estuary in Courseulles-sur-Mer whereas the *GR. 726* held the sector stretching as far as Grandcamp-Maisy. Oberst Walter Korfes, commander of the *GR. 726*, had his command post established in the Château de Sully near Bayeux. Five companies were in charge of defending the sector stretching from Pointe du Hoc to Sainte-Honorine-des-Pertes.

Colonel Wilhelm Ritcher photographed before his promotion to the rank of General in command of the *716. ID.* © Mémorial de Caen

Turkoman soldiers studying a relief map of the coast in the autumn of 1943. © Bundesarchiv

THE GERMAN DEFENCES ON OMAHA

The Beach of the Golden Sands was defended by 13 resistance nests. They made the most of the terrain and were capable of driving back assaults from all directions and of offering support to neighbouring positions. The firing range offered by the shoreline enabled both raking and cross-firing.

To the east, *WN 60*, located on the high plateau that overlooks the dell referred to as La Révolution, was equipped with a 75mm howitzer, 4 tobruks for mortar, a tank turret and several machine guns. *WN 61*, established at the foot of the same plateau, was a lighter position, but comprised a 50mm Pak 38 gun and a formidable 88mm *Pak 43/41* sheltered by a casemate. *WN 62*, located to the west, was the most powerful strongpoint, along with *WN 72*, in terms of firing power. They included two casemates with Czech *Skoda* 76.5mm howitzers and a 50mm antitank gun. An antitank ditch blocked the access to the valley.

WN 64 and *WN 65*, controlling access to the Ruquet valley, were never completed. They were equipped with a Soviet 76.2mm gun and three 50mm pieces housed in casemates. A 75mm piece installed within a log shelter raked the road leading to Saint-Laurent. *WN 66* and *WN 68* were established where the Moulins valley leading to Saint-Laurent opens out and stretched out as far as the beach. Heavy weapons were concentrated in the narrowest zone: one 47mm and two 50mm antitank guns. *WN 67* and *WN 67a* (69), located slightly inland to the west of Saint-Laurent, housed thirty-eight 320mm *Nebelwerfer 40/41* ("fog thrower") rocket launch ramps belonging to the *Nebelwerfer* Regiment 84, one 50mm *Pak 38* antitank gun and one Flak. *WN 68*, under construction, was equipped with two *Ringstands* for armoured turrets and two 50mm guns. *WN 70, 71, 72* and *73*, defending access to the Vierville valley, formed a powerful defensive position. An 88m antitank gun, a French 75mm gun and a further 50mm gun raked the beach. The casemate that housed the first was built on the site of the former Hôtel Legallois.

WN 63, established in Colleville-sur-Mer, served as an underground command post and radio station for the 3rd company of the *Infanterie Regiment 726*. Striking antitank ditches were hollowed out at the exits of the Moulins valleys in Saint-Laurent and

German Gr.W.34 80mm mortar.
© Omaha Beach Memorial Museum

Metal case for a 50mm Gr.W.36 mortar shell.
© VD Collection.

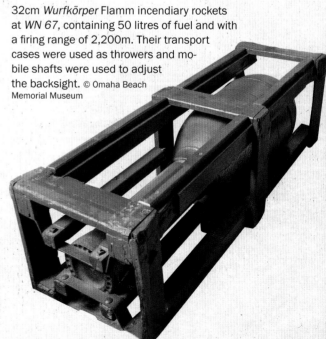

32cm *Wurfkörper* Flamm incendiary rockets at *WN 67*, containing 50 litres of fuel and with a firing range of 2,200m. Their transport cases were used as throwers and mobile shafts were used to adjust the backsight. © Omaha Beach Memorial Museum

STRONGPOINTS AND RESISTANCE NESTS

The Atlantic Wall relied on 4 models of defensive organisation: the "defence zone" (*Verteidigungsbereiche*), the "group of strongpoints" (*Stützpunktgruppe*), the "strongpoints" (*Stützpunkte*) defending a limited coastal sector and the "resistance nests" (*Widerstandsnester*) which comprised the first level of coastal defence.

A *WN* was generally comprised of one or two casemates equipped with mid-calibre antitank guns (50, 75 or 88mm), a tobruk for rapid fire machine guns and mortar, a gun emplacement surmounted with a tank turret and one or several light anti-aircraft pieces (20 or 37mm guns) and, occasionally, projectors. The position was completed with a shelter for troops, a command post and ammunition holds. Networks of barbed wire, minefields and, sometimes, automatic flamethrowers surrounded the position. Other networks of (zigzagging) underground or open-air trenches enabled soldiers to circulate under cover.

Vierville. Two metre-high zigzagged antitank walls blocked the access to both valleys. Further west, Pointe de la Percée housed *WN 74*. Two old Czech *Skoda* 76.5mm howitzers installed under a log roof could fire over the beach.

A total of 18 antitank guns, 3 howitzers, 3 light Flak pieces, 15 mortars, 9 tank turrets and 85 machine guns dispersed their firing power over the beaches, ensuring the close-range defence of strongpoints.

Tobruk surmounted by a Panzer IV turret at *WN 68*.
© NARA

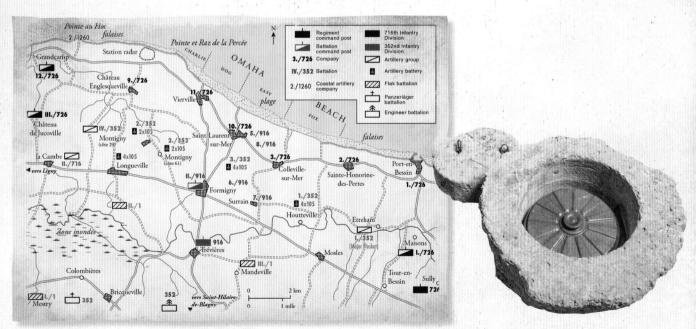

Organisation of German forces in the Omaha sector on 6th June 1944.

Tellermine housed in concrete.
© Omaha Beach Memorial Museum

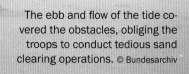

The ebb and flow of the tide covered the obstacles, obliging the troops to conduct tedious sand clearing operations. © Bundesarchiv

ACHTUNG MINEN -

On the beach and around the defensive perimeter of the strongpoints and batteries, German pioneer units disseminated thousands of land mines of all sorts. Antitank mines, *Tellerminen*, were used against vehicles and tanks, but also against barges. The Germans had produced antipersonnel mines that were particularly insidious and deadly.

In order to render them difficult to detect, they used amagnetic materials. The *Stockmine* was a traction mine made of a concrete cylinder filled with metal splinters and mounted on a wooden stake; the *Glassmine M43* was a glass pressure mine that looked like a simple jam pot. The *Holzmine* was a small and rudimentary wooden box, but it

was enough to blow a man's foot off. Nicknamed Bouncing Betty by the GIs, the *Schutzenmine 35* was undoubtedly the most terrible of all. When the mechanism entered into action, the mine bounced 1.5 metres up in the air to explode, sending 350 steel balls over a radius of 100 metres.

To further increase their destructive capacity, they were connected together with wires and their firing systems were infinitely modified by extremely ingenious and perfidious pioneers. Certain weapons were booby-trapped for delayed-action explosion or even during defusing. Along the clifftops, navy shells were suspended in such a manner that they could be dropped on assailants.

Glassminen. These glass mines were impossible to detect and inexpensive to produce. © VD Collection

Wooden sign warning of the presence of a minefield. © Mémorial de Caen

S-35Mine, nicknamed Bouncing Betty. © Mémorial de Caen

THE BEACH OBSTACLES

Rommel ordered for the troops defending the coast to install lines of obstacles along the shoreline that would be submerged at high tide. They were designed to put flat-bottomed barges out of action, to overturn them or to cause them serious damage. For this astute tactician expected the Allies to land at high tide in order to limit the distance to be run without cover against enemy assault units. He nevertheless considered a low-tide landing and had new lines of obstacles set up accordingly.

The German troops began to install them in May, requisitioning local inhabitants to accelerate the pace. The first line of obstruction, almost permanently submerged, was composed of Cointet- or C-elements, also referred to as "Belgian gates", comprised of metal bars mounted on 3 metre-wide and 2.5 metre-high rollers of a weight of 1.4 tonnes. Then, sloping obstruction beams (*Hemmbalken*) were installed. They were of a height of 3 to 4 metres and were mounted on a bipod. Steel blades with saw teeth or antitank mines attached to their summits enabled them to rip open the hulls of passing vessels or to overturn them. Over 2,000 wooden

The tetrahedron, also known as the Czech hedgehog, was used in large numbers, essentially but not only to protect Czech frontiers and fortification lines. The shape and robustness of this welded steel obstacle was particularly efficient against tanks. © Omaha Beach Memorial Museum

stakes facing out to sea, some of which were surmounted with *Tellerminen* (*Hölzpfähle*), completed the defensive system. Around thirty metres away, tetrahedrons (*Tschechenigel*), also referred to as Czech hedgehogs, comprised an assembly of three welded steel beams or portions of railing set on a concrete base.

The C-element, designed by Colonel Cointet de Fillain, was used in 1939 by the Belgian army to prevent vehicles from passing. The 74,000 C-elements produced were recovered by the *Wehrmacht* and transformed into beach obstacles. © Big Red One Museum

NEWCOMERS

Generalleutnant Dietrich Kraiss's *352. Infanterie Division* joined the Saint-Lô sector in February 1944. The unit, created near Hanover late 1943, comprised 12,700 men, including 6,800 combatants and 1,500 volunteer Russian auxiliaries *(Hiwis)*. It was the most powerful infantry unit deployed in Normandy.

It benefited from experienced supervision. A great number of officers and non-commissioned officers were from units that had been disbanded after having been bled dry on the Eastern Front. The vast majority of troops were young conscripts and Ukrainian, Georgian and Belarusian volunteers. The *726. IR* and the *Ost-Bataillon 439* which belonged to the *716. ID* were placed under Kraiss's tactical command. The division, at full staff, included 3 infantry divisions, one artillery regiment and one engineering battalion, but also a bicycle reconnaissance battalion and a powerful antitank unit. It was equipped with large quantities of heavy weapons; however, lacked ammunition, vehicles and fuel.

On the 15th of March 1944, Rommel gave orders to transfer division artillery to the coast in order to reinforce the *716. ID*. Ultimately, the *352. ID* would be required to ensure, alone, the defence of the coastal zone stretching from the River Vire to the north of Bayeux. Kraiss established his command post in Le Molay-Littry, in the centre of the sector covered by his division. He kept a vast share of his unit inland in order to drive back any potential enemy penetration. His units could nevertheless reach the coast in a relatively short timescale.

The *GR. 916* commanded by *Oberst* Goth covered the coastal zone stretching from Colleville-sur-Mer to Grandcamp. The *III. Bataillon* was deployed to the west of Vierville, whilst the *II. Bataillon* was in charge of the Beach of the Golden Sands. One 150mm and three 105mm howitzer batteries were positioned just over a mile behind the beach. Artillery lookouts were posted in coastal bunkers to direct battery firing.

Generalleutnant Dietrich Kraiss. His division retreated foot by foot, fiercely defending Saint-Lô. It was declared out of action late July 1944. Kraiss was wounded on the 4th of August and died two days later. © Bundesarchiv

Insignia of the *352. Infanterie Division*.

INFORMATION THAT ARRIVED TOO LATE TO CHANGE PLANS

Information regarding movements by elements belonging to the *352. ID* in the vicinity of the Bessin coast was forwarded to the US and British intelligence services via Ultra and the French Resistance. Montgomery was informed by his intelligence officer, Brigadier General E.T. "Bill" William. It was also mentioned in the 21st Army Group's weekly summary dated 3rd May 1944. News of the redeployment of the entire German division to the rear of the Omaha and Gold sectors reached the Allies; however, far too late for them to modify their plans and to prepare for such a threat. At this point, forwarding the information to combatants would only have weakened their morale and their fighting spirit.

Leather map case belonging to a *Heer* officer and a pair of 6x30 binoculars. © VD Collection

Wounded soldiers' insignia

THE SACRIFICE MADE BY THE RESISTANCE

As was the case elsewhere, a small Resistance group was in operation in the Saint-Laurent-sur-Mer sector. Georges Thomine, a fisherman from Port-en-Bessin was in charge of intelligence for the sector. He worked for the Alliance network in association with the Intelligence Service. Created in November 1940 by the commander Loustaunau-Lacau, alias "Navarre", it was one of the most active intelligence networks along with Colonel Rémy's Confrérie Notre-Dame. In January 1943, he recruited Désiré Lemière and Charles Olard, the stand-in postman and the postmaster from the Saint-Laurent post office, together with Robert Boulard, also a postman in Trévières. The 3 men collected information on the German defences' progression on the Bessin coast.

However, in the spring of 1944, the Alliance network was infiltrated and partly disbanded by the *Abwehr*. Robert Douin, the *département* chief, Georges Thomine and several other Resistance members were arrested by the Caen Gestapo in March. The Saint-Laurent cell was apprehended in turn on the 5th of May. Désiré Lemière was arrested in front of his wife and children.

On the 6th of June, when D-Day was announced, *Hauptmann* Hoffmann, commander of the German quarter of Caen prison, was to execute the orders he had received in the case of alert. That very morning, he was to send to Germany all prisoners relating to the Gestapo to avoid they fall into the hands of the Allies. Prisoners pending *Wehrmacht* court judgment were, depending on the seriousness of accusations against them, either to be deported to Germany or to be immediately set free. These orders were confirmed by the *Feldkommandantur*; however, bombardments had rendered the railway station in Caen totally unfit for use. The Germans had neither the necessary trucks nor men to evacuate the 87 *Nacht und Nebel* ("Night and Fog") prisoners. At around 8 in the morning, Harald Heyns, the Gestapo chief, went to the prison and told Hoffman that the prisoners were to be immediately executed. From dawn to dusk, they were taken in groups of 6 to a small courtyard inside the prison to be put to death.

Désiré Lemière, Albert Anne, Robert Boulard and Charles Olard were among the victims. The women's quarter was not spared. Twenty prisoners were transferred to Fresnes. Their bodies were then buried in hastily hollowed out ditches in the 4 neighbouring courtyards and were covered with lime. Late June, the Germans came back to exhume the bodies to take them to a place that remains unknown to this very day.

Portrait of Désiré Lemière.
© DR

Désirée Lemière's wedding photograph.
© Oxéant family collection.

Staff from the 5th Engineer Special Brigade boarding LCVP 497, which took them to *USS Thurston* (AP-77). © NARA

CHAPTER 2

FROM THE OTHER SIDE OF THE CHANNEL

LANDING IN FRANCE

The idea of a landing operation on the western European coastline very quickly appealed to the US high command. Under the leadership of the army Chief of Staff George C. Marshall, the War Plans Division devised 2 projects for amphibious operations in order to immobilise German divisions, hence relieving the Red Army. The first operation, codenamed *Sledgehammer*, involved landing on the Cotentin peninsula in September 1942. The second, codenamed *Round Up* and involving 48 divisions, was planned for the spring of 1943 between Boulogne and Le Havre. Although well aware of the decisive nature a direct attack on Germany may have, the British deemed such action premature, due to their lack of experience and to the military weakness of both nations at this point in the conflict.

The ground was prepared during the Quadrant (Quebec) and Trident (Washington) conferences. The invasion was scheduled to take place on the north-western French coast on the 1st of May 1944. The Chief of Staff to Supreme Allied Commander (COSSAC) was in charge of preparing Operation Overlord. It was up to him to decide on the broad lines of the landing operation and to select the future assault zone. The decision came in June 1943. It was to be Normandy. During the Teheran conference on the 28th of November, Churchill, Roosevelt and Stalin approved the proposals put forward by the COSSAC. Appointed commander in chief of the Allied forces in Europe, General David Dwight Eisenhower arrived in England on the 14th of January 1944, with the mission to set up the Supreme Headquarter Allied Expeditionary Force (SHAEF) and to have the Anglo-American troops land in Normandy to achieve the final victory that would lead them to the Reich.

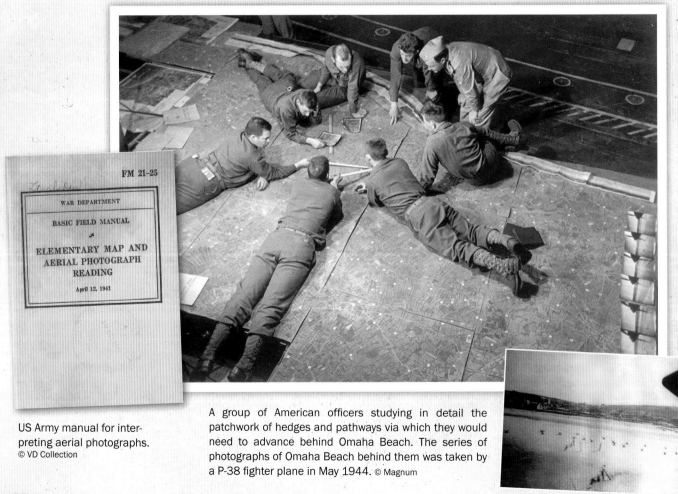

US Army manual for interpreting aerial photographs.
© VD Collection

A group of American officers studying in detail the patchwork of hedges and pathways via which they would need to advance behind Omaha Beach. The series of photographs of Omaha Beach behind them was taken by a P-38 fighter plane in May 1944. © Magnum

PREPARATIONS

Over the following months, Great Britain was transformed into a gigantic military camp. Around 3.5 million soldiers, of several nationalities, were posted across the British countryside. They trained relentlessly whilst the high command perfected its battle plans. Tens of thousands of tanks, trucks and guns were gathered in open-air storage areas, along with ammunition, food and fuel. Thirteen thousand planes of all sorts were lined up on the airfield tarmacs as far as the eye could see. Over 1,300 warships, 1,600 merchant ships from the United States, the Pacific and the Mediterranean were anchored off shore and around 4,000 landing barges were lined along the docks in ports.

British-made SHAEF insignia. © VD Collection

OPERATION BOLERO

A landing operation on the western European coastline would require sending a sizeable American expeditionary force to Great Britain. This painstaking operation was codenamed *Bolero* in reference to the crescendo of the famous opera by Maurice Ravel. The invasion was impossible before July 1943, given the time needed for the United States to prepare militarily and to produce the necessary equipment for such large-scale offensive action.

GIs from the 29th US Infantry Division on the deck of LST *Queen Mary*.

The transfer began in April 1942, but was to slow down. The lack of ships, the threat posed by packs of enemy submarines in the Atlantic and the despatching of part of the expeditionary corps to the Mediterranean were to hinder the growth of the one destined to be posted in Great Britain. On the 31st of July 1943, only 238,000 GIs were stationed in the United Kingdom; however, the defeat of the *U-Boote* enabled the pace to be accelerated. Around 700,000 men crossed the Atlantic in just 6 months. By May 1944, their numbers had increased to 1,527,000.

Hundreds of merchant ships were mobilised within the context of Operation Bolero. Hence, the British liner *RMS Queen Mary*, winner of the Blue Riband in 1936 and 1938, was transformed into a troop transport ship. After several crossings to Australia the Old Lady, as she was commonly referred to, was used to take GIs to British soil before the landing operation in Normandy. The liner's dimensions enabled it to transport some 15,000 men and its speed of 30 knots was an asset for avoiding the German submarines. In September 1942, the 29th Infantry Division crossed the Atlantic aboard a liner. Winston Churchill was later to say that the Allies had won the war thanks to the *Queen Mary*.

RMS Queen Mary life jacket.
© Mémorial de Caen

REVISING THE PLAN

The Allies had finally opted for Normandy. The site seemed to satisfy all the conditions propitious to an amphibious assault. The low beaches were sufficiently wide and accessible to enable the simultaneous landing of several divisions. Furthermore, they were sheltered from prevailing winds by the Cotentin peninsula and the inland area was suitable for establishing airfields and deploying armoured units. Although further away from England, the Normandy coast offered the advantage of being potentially isolated from the rest of France by blocking the bridges over the Seine and the Loire. Once the bridgeheads had been consolidated, the Allied armies would be able to spread out their deployment across France.

Beyond these strategic advantages, the coast was poorly fortified, offered long beaches and 2 deep-water ports: Cherbourg on one side and Le Havre on the other; Cherbourg – the weak German coastal defence in the area also weighed heavily in the Allied command's final choice.

The COSSAC project originally recommended an amphibious assault involving 3 infantry divisions (one American and two British) and one airborne division over a 40km-wide front stretching from Saint-Aubin-sur-Mer to Vierville-sur-Mer. The 3 chosen beaches were codenamed Juno, Gold and Omaha. However, the SHAEF feared that the narrowness of the front and the weakness of

Eisenhower and Montgomery having talks shortly before D-Day.
© NARA

Air-launched flyer distributed on 29th December announcing Eisenhower's appointment in command of the second front. © VD Collection

Guide issued to GIs stationed in Great Britain. © VD Collection

General Eisenhower and the complete SHAEF staff. © NARA

the assault force may jeopardise the operation. The assault sector was extended on both sides. Two new beaches were added: Sword, stretching from Lion-sur-Mer to Ouistreham and Utah from Saint-Martin-de-Varreville to Sainte-Marie-du-Mont. General Miles Dempsey's 2nd British Army was in charge of the eastern assault sector, whereas the 2 beaches located to the west, Omaha and Utah, were placed under the responsibility of General Omar Bradley's 1st US Army.

This change implied a longer timescale to rally round the extra men and materials required. As such, the landing was postponed from early May to early June. Several imperatives determined the choice of "D-Day": a full moon to help parachutists, followed by a dawn assault, at mid rising tide in order to avoid the traps Rommel had installed on the beaches. Consequently, the date was set at 5th June, with possible postponement to the 6th or 7th.

Major General Leonard T. Gerow, who had been promoted in July 1943 as commander of the V US Army Corps, was considered to be one of the best military chiefs in the American army. Along with his troops, he was entrusted with the task of launching the assault on Omaha before joining the British troops to the east and the US VII Corps to the west. The following units were at his disposal: the 1st, 29th and 2nd US Infantry Divisions. A Provisional Ranger Force, comprised of the 2nd and

5th Rangers Battalions was incorporated within the 29th US Infantry Division. The units selected to take part in the amphibious assault on Omaha were ready at last.

Omar Bradley meeting with General Gerow, commander of the V US Army Corps, and Major General Gerhardt, commander of the 29th US Infantry Division. © US Army

PRECIOUS ALLIES

On the opposite shores of the English Channel, intelligence specialists painstakingly scrutinised low altitude pictures of the Omaha sector and matched any resulting information with that provided by the Resistance. Analysts compared pictures with older ones in order to monitor the progression of fortification work. They could clearly distinguish the different types of construction. All these details were copied onto maps which were to be used on D-Day and during the Battle of Normandy. A special BIGOT stamp was placed on all these ultra secret documents. This codename was a reversal of To Gib (to Gibraltar) which was stamped on documents pertaining to the Allied landings in North Africa in November 1942. Other specialised maps were produced for certain units, specifically based on their mission and their specialisation. The German troops never had any such maps; however, thanks to their knowledge of the terrain and their tactical skills, they

nevertheless gave the American troops an extremely hard time during the Battle of Normandy.

This extremely rare American map was found in La Ferté Macé in 2015. The first side represents the physical region of Normandy at a scale of 1/250,000; the second is more original and offers a general outline of the region as seen from England. Roadways, waterways, forests and flooded zones are all represented. General information on the country and the military principles to abide by are written on the border. In the lower left corner, an oblique view highlights the relief on Omaha Beach as far as hill 192, which controlled the town of Saint-Lô. This highly specific information and the place the map was discovered offer proof that it was used by an officer from the Big Red One, a unit that was posted in La Ferté Macé from the 18th to the 23rd of August 1944.

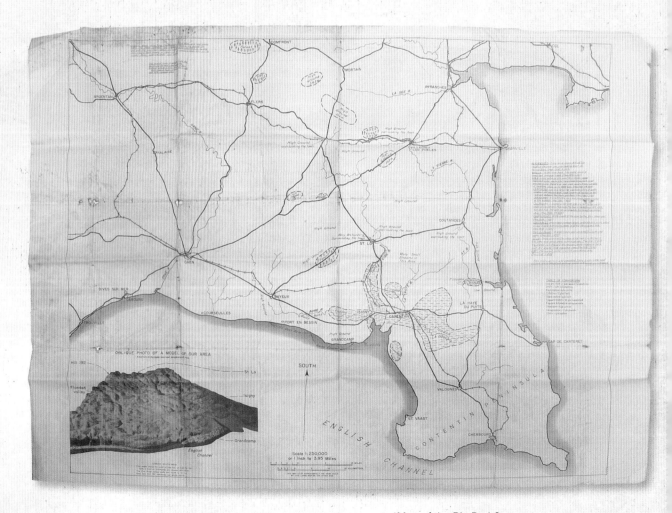

Map of the Big Red One. © F. Normand Collection

THE BIG RED ONE

The 1st US Infantry Division, the famous Big Red One, was one of the US Army's most experienced divisions and its motto, *"No Mission Too Difficult, No Sacrifice Too Great—Duty First"* was well deserved. The unit, which gained fame during the Great War, brilliantly accomplished all the missions it was entrusted with. It landed in Oran, in Algeria, on the 8th of November 1942 (Operation Torch), before being engaged in Tunisia, then taking part in a second amphibious operation in Sicily (Operation Husky). The division had been in intensive training in England since October 1943. Major General Clarence Huebner led his men with a firm hand to ensure they could face any unexpected situation. The unit declared itself to be the best commanded and the best trained. Its emblem, a red figure "1" is an obvious sign of this frame of mind.

Colonel Taylor's 16th RCT was first to land to the east of Omaha Beach, in the Easy and Fox sectors. The 18th then the 26th RCT arrived as of mid-morning to advance southwards and towards Arromanches to make the junction with the British troops.

These documents retrace the career of a lieutenant from the 16th Infantry Regiment. This leather wallet, a souvenir of his travels to North Africa, contains a picture of his fiancée. He has preciously kept the guides distributed during the amphibious operations codenamed Husky and Neptune, together with his invasion money. The 2nd and 1st Lieutenant ranks prove that he was promoted. The division insignia was produced in Great Britain. © VD Collection

Major General Clarence Huebner replaced Terry Allen in charge of the Big Red One in 1943. © DR

"We very quickly learned that we would be part of D-Day, at H-Hour and that we would be the first assault wave. It was no surprise given our preparation up till then... We had studied scale models of our landing zone made of earth and sand. We had also identified the beach exits that needed to be secured and our initial target, the village of Colleville-sur-Mer, on the Normandy coast. Our beach had been codenamed Omaha, and our landing sector was called Easy Red. There were enlargements of photographic details, taken by the P38s during hedgehopping flights: they showed the stretches of beach at low tide, the obstacles in the water and on the beach and lots of kids busy working, obviously surprised. The initially planned date of the 5th of June was postponed to the 6th of June because of bad weather and because it was the day the tide would be lowest over the coming months. This low spring tide would also ensure that the majority of the obstacles and mines placed in the water would be visible."

Sergeant Donald Wilson, 1st US Infantry Division, 16th Regiment, Company F.

Infantrymen from the 1st US Infantry Division on an English beach. Royal Navy LCAs can be seen in the background. © NARA

THE BLUE AND GRAY

The 29th US Infantry Division, engaged alongside the 1st, was a traditional unit that had distinguished itself during the War of Independence against the British. The Blue and Gray was part of the National Guard and entered into active service in February 1941, to be transferred to the United Kingdom in October 1942. It essentially comprised national guards from Virginia, Maryland and the district of Colombia. The division's insignia, a blue and grey Korean Yin and Yang reminds us of the unit's mixed composition and its history. Gerow was replaced in July 1943 by Major General Charles H. Gerhardt. Although respected, Gerhardt was hated by many of his men for his extremely strict sense of discipline. The 29th US Infantry Division was well-trained and experienced in amphibious exercises. Its morale was excellent, yet few of its soldiers had combat experience. Gerhardt improved his unit's cohesion by integrating men from the 29th Rangers Battalion who had been trained by British commandos.

Major General H. Gerhardt replaced Leonard T. Gerow in command of the division in July 1943. He was a strict disciplinarian and was extremely demanding with his men.
© Rights Reserved

Colonel Canham's 116th RCT, with support from the 5th Rangers, was the first to endure its baptism of fire. The team was to take control of the Dog sector running from Vierville to the locality of Les Moulins. After clearing the last pockets of resistance around Omaha, the 115th and 175th RCTs were to walk to Isigny and Carentan to make the junction with the US VII Corps.

Men from the 29th US Infantry Division in training in Dartmoor. © Mémorial de Caen

Division insignia surmounted with the title of the 29th Rangers.
© VD Collection

Pineapple grenade for instruction. © VD Collection

"You have been chosen by the SHAEF to take part in one of the most important military operations in History. Your task will be to destroy the Nazi forces defending the gate to Western Europe and to take our forces, victorious, to Berlin. The way has been paved. The Hun has been chased from the seas, demolished by the Russians, driven out of Africa, bombarded from the airs and he is waiting, nervous and desperate, for us to make the final blow. You are well prepared for this job. No troop has ever been so well trained, and so superbly equipped. To support us, there will be formidable Allied naval and aerial forces. Success is guaranteed. And victory will bring the eternal gratitude of liberated nations across the globe. I have total confidence in your capacity, your courage and your determination. Hit hard and continue to move forward. We will fight with God by our sides and we cannot lose. Good luck to each and every one of you."

Major General Gerow's speech to his men, 18th May 1944.

USM1 heavy helmet with the insignia of the 29th US Infantry Division.
© P. Cage Collection

Aerial photograph of Vierville.

THE RANGERS

A Provisional Ranger Force, comprised of the 2nd and 5th Rangers Battalions was incorporated within the 29th US Infantry Division. It was to ensure the protection of the right flank of the 116th RCT and to capture Pointe du Hoc, whose guns had a firing range of 25km and could consequently reach the landing fleets anchored off-shore of Omaha and Utah. Trained in the United States in 1943, the 2nd and 5th Rangers Battalions were comprised of volunteers from all branches of the US Army. These units were directly inspired by British commandos

Badges of the 2nd and the 5th Rangers. These British Army insignia remind us that the Rangers were trained by her Majesty's commandos. © VD Collection

and were subjected to the same preparation. Members deemed to be too weak were excluded from the unit. On the 2nd of April, the 2 battalions left the United states for Scotland.

"Three old women with brooms could keep the Rangers from climbing that cliff."

Colonel Cleveland Lytle's Force A reunited Companies D, E and F, for a total of 225 men. The force was to scale the cliff of Pointe du Hoc, destroy the guns there and advance inland to cut the coastal road linking Grandcamp-les-Bains and Vierville. The Rangers were to hold out until the arrival of troops landed on Omaha. Captain Ralph Goranson's Company C formed Force B. It was to land on Omaha Beach, to the west of Vierville, walk westwards to neutralise the radar station at Pointe de la Percée; then head for Pointe du Hoc. Finally, Force C, reuniting Lieutenant Colonel Schneider's

5th Rangers and the 2nd Rangers' Companies A and B were, depending on the situation on Pointe du Hoc, either to be directly taken there or to be landed in the Dog Green sector and to head to their target from inland by following the coast road. If necessary, they would reinforce the 116th RCT.

Rangers in training. In February 1944, they trained intensively over two weeks, climbing the Needles, a series of chalky cliffs on the Isle of Wight. On their return, any soldiers and officers who failed to satisfy conditions were excluded. © NARA

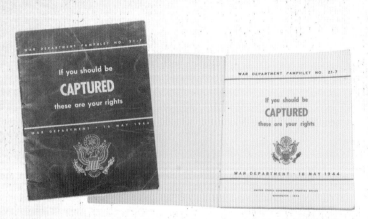

Manual including the information required in the case of capture by the enemy. © VD Collection

Thompson submachine gun. Its .45 ACP ammunition offered it unrivalled stopping power. © Mémorial de Caen

A flamethrower team simulating an attack on a bunker during a training session. © US Army

An Assault Boat Team advancing in close order through a specially prepared corridor. © US Army

WOOLACOMBE

The units chosen to participate in the amphibious assault were subjected to intensive training. Walks, physical training, exercises, theoretical and practical lessons were maintained at a highly intense pace. Discipline was strict, for the men needed to be ready. Their commitment was in line with the missions they were to accomplish.

As from September 1943, all units participated in a training course of several weeks at Lieutenant-Colonel Paul Thompson's Assault Training Centre. The centre was established in Woolacombe and was used to train American combat units on landing techniques up to regiment level. Each feature of the Atlantic Wall was carefully studied in order to devise the best way to neutralise or destroy it. Special equipment and explosive

devices were regularly tested. The Engineers produced rudimentary models of barges to enable assault teams to take up positions and to get out as quickly as possible. Networks of barbed wire, bunkers and obstacles were built to familiarise combatants. Infantrymen learned how to place Bangalore torpedoes under barbed wire, how to fire bazookas into bunker embrasures, to use flamethrowers or to place pole charges against concrete fortifications. Gunners learned how to use their artillery pieces from the bridge of their vessels, mechanics learned how to waterproof the mechanical devices on vehicles using magnetic

Woolacombe training centre. © DR

paste and they installed air intake and ducts and exhausts so that they could move in water. Units received tactical and technical training designed to enable them to fulfil their mission in perfect coordination with the other forces engaged on D-Day.

The American naval forces, who had taken part in amphibious exercises in the United States, also had training centres in Salcombe, Milford Haven and Appledore. They contributed towards training the US Army in order to accustom soldiers to assembly, boarding and landing procedures.

THE REGIMENTAL COMBAT TEAM

Experience acquired during amphibious operations had led the American high command to realise that a standard infantry unit alone could not accomplish certain missions. They consequently composed specialised regimental units to lead the assault on the beaches: Regimental Combat Teams (RCT). Each infantry regiment had its own tank battalion, two motorised artillery battalions, one engineering battalion, one anti-aircraft battalion, a medical detachment and a heavy mortar company. All these units were placed under the direct orders of the regiment chief. Out in the field, sapper detachments could be dispersed among different regimental units for, amidst the fury and the confusion of combat, their small size facilitated command whilst offering sufficient firing power. Once their operations were complete, these units were returned to the army corps. The RCTs were to support the weight of the battle until reinforcements arrived.

A Captain from the 29th USID taking his men through a barbed wire curtain.
© Mémorial de Caen

MAJOR EXERCISES

The units selected to launch the assault on the Normandy beaches received tactical and technical training designed to enable them to fulfil their mission in perfect coordination with the other forces engaged on D-Day.

However, the high command was keen to put each and every assault force to the test in order to perfect their preparation and inter-army cooperation, which was crucial for this type of operation. The naval and air forces, service units, infantry and combat engineers, the artillery and tanks were all summoned to practice major manoeuvres at Slapton Sands on the Devonshire coast. The exercise codenamed Duck and organised in January yielded many lessons. Force O took part in the Fox and Smash exercises. The Fabius exercise, reuniting all 5 assault forces, was their ultimate rehearsal. The 1st and 29th US Infantry Divisions and the two ESB brigades were deployed within the context of Fabius I.

English children watching a landing exercise on a small beach in Devon. © NARA

Pot of Asbestos Compound found in Normandy. This product was used to render the mechanisms aboard amphibious vehicles watertight. © Big Red One Museum

Tank Destroyer M10 tanks heading for the sand. Rolls of wire mesh are ready to be installed to avoid them becoming blocked in the sand. © NARA

Manoeuvres at Slapton Sands.
© NARA

The wrecked stern of LST 289 after a torpedo attack by an *S-Boot*. © NARA

But the enemy was near. On the evening of the 27th of April, two Force U convoys left Plymouth and Brixham to take part in exercise Tiger. The T-4 convoy transporting the 1st Engineer Special Brigade was intercepted by a flotilla of 9 German motor torpedo boats on its way from Cherbourg. Although detected during their approach, the *Landing Ship Tanks could not be informed*. The corvette *HMS Azalea* which served as the convoy's escort, was no match. Two LSTs were sunk and two others were seriously damaged. The sea was strewn with castaways. A total of 198 seamen and 551 infantrymen were killed. Ten Bigot officers were among the dead, however, their secret was safe.

LCM and LCI approaching the beach. © NARA

ASSAULT BARGES

In 1944, the Allied navies boasted a range of specialised flat bottomed vessels of varying tonnages that enabled them to launch several amphibious operations in the Pacific and the Mediterranean. Certain barges were reserved for use by the infantry, whereas others could transport wheeled vehicles or even tanks. The Allied planners were going to be faced with great difficulty in reuniting the necessary number of barges for Operation Neptune. But they met the challenge and, on the 6th of June, the barges, of American and British design took the American troops towards the Normandy beaches.

Landing Craft Assault (LCA)

These small, British-designed barges with a low draught were originally intended for commando operations. Their speed never exceeded 8 knots. In contrast with other barges, the steering compartment was located at the bow. The hull was made of counterveneer and was reinforced with armoured plating. The LCA transported 30 to 35 men, seated inside in 3 rows. They left the vessel via a double armoured door and a narrow ramp located at the bow. The Rangers from the 116th RCT were taken to Omaha aboard LCAs.

US Navy deck jacket.
© VD Collection

Rangers familiarising themselves with British LCAs. © NARA

Landing Craft Infantry Large (LCI)

This heavy landing barge could transport 200 soldiers and 32 tonnes of equipment. Although fast and manoeuvrable, the LCI(L) offered relatively mediocre seaworthiness due to its wide flat bottom. Troops were disembarked via mobile ramps that were located on either side of the hull. The Americans used several specialised versions: the LCI(G) for Gunboat, the LCI(M) for Mortar, the LCI(R) for Rocket and the LC(FF) for Flotilla Flagship, a command ship.

© NARA

© NARA

Landing Craft Mechanized (LCM)

This barge had a sufficient payload to house a mid-sized 30-tonne tank, to help reinforce the first waves of assault. It was in fact a motorised pontoon with flat sides and a wheelhouse cabin to the stern. The Mk 2, 3 and 6 models were built by the firm Higgins in New Orleans, whilst the Mk 4 and 6 models were assembled in Great Britain. LCMs were used to transport engineering platoons and their equipment towards Omaha.

Landing Craft Tank (LCT)

The LCT was designed to transport tanks. Its welded steel hull rendered the barge extremely robust, well capable of crossing the English Channel and of withstanding several groundings. The British LCT Mk 4, of a length of 57 metres, was used on the Normandy coast. The US Navy used 2 models of more modest dimensions and capable of transporting five 30-tonne tanks or four 50-tonne tanks. The Mk 5 was equipped with one single hinged ramp to the bow, whereas the Mk 6 also had a gate to the stern, for transhipment out at sea with LSTs and for unloading material on dry land.

© NARA

THE HIGGINS BOAT

For the design of his Landing Craft Vehicle & Personnel, Andrew Higgins sought inspiration from the shape of the vessels that sailed over the Louisiana marshes. Over 20,000 boats left the Higgins Industries naval construction yards in New Orleans.

The LCVP was built entirely of wood and could transport a platoon of 36 men with their equipment or 1 jeep and 12 men, at a speed of 9 knots. For long crossings, it was transported on davits aboard troop transport ships. It had two machine gun emplacements to the stern, a sheltered steering compartment and a radio. The LCVP was a manoeuvrable vessel that could be grounded to ensure the rapid landing of its load and return out to sea without assistance thanks to its v-shaped hull. The tip-up ramp located to the bow was the boat's only armoured feature. The assault infantry was generally taken to Omaha aboard LCPVs; however, certain units, the rangers in particular, used Royal Navy Landing Craft Assault barges.

Front of an LCVP. © Omaha Beach Memorial Museum

© Magnum

43

OPERATION GAMBIT

On New Year's Day in 1944, team n°1 from the Combined Operations Assault Pilotage Party, comprised of Major Logan Scott-Bowden from the Royal Engineers and Sergeant Bruce Ogden-Smith, secretly left Gosport aboard a launch. They landed near Ver-sur-Mer to take measurements and samples of sand using an auger, in order to ensure that armoured vehicles could be unloaded onto Gold Beach. The two men returned to Newhaven safe and sound with their precious load. Their mission had met with total success. Shortly afterwards, the American military command was duly informed and called upon the COPP to obtain as much information as possible on Omaha Beach.

The mission was to last several days and the operating procedure was modified accordingly. This time, the COPP team was to be transported by X-Craft midget submarine. On the 16th of January 1944, *HMS X-20*, commanded by Lieutenant Ken Hudspeth from the Royal Australian Naval Volunteer Reserve (RANVR), was towed offshore of the Normandy coast. Its 3-man crew shared the narrow cockpit with Scott-Bowden and Ogden-Smith. They had been entrusted with the mission of drawing up an accurate map of the seabed, of studying currents and tides and of observing defences through the periscope. The submersible worked for 2 days off the shores of Luc-sur-Mer, before heading west towards Port-en-Bessin, to the same beach here Major March-Phillipps' commando had been taken by surprise and annihilated 15 months earlier. The COPP troops donned their diving suits and swam 400 metres to the beach. They had to work whilst avoiding patrols and projector beams. They took deep-water measurements using a lead line. By day, the men scrutinised the coast through the

Fairbairn Sykes dagger used by the British commandos.
© Mémorial de Caen

The X-Craft was a small 15.5 metre-long submersible with neither cabin nor weapons. It was designed for reconnaissance, mining and sabotage missions in shallow waters near the coast.
© Wikipedia / Geni

periscope, swallowing quantities of benzedrine, an amphetamine, to keep awake. It was impossible for them to stay standing or to lie down. After 4 days, the bad weather and fatigue forced Hudspeth to put a stop to the mission. The totally exhausted crew was taken back to England aboard *HMS Dolphin*.

Upon his arrival, Scott-Bowden presented his report to an audience of British and American generals and admirals. When Bradley questioned him on Omaha, he was categorical. There were major risks and losses would by no means be comparable with those in other sectors. Thanks to the mission's results, 2 scale models of the beaches were produced. The first was installed in room 474 at the Metropol Hotel, a room occupied by the War Department, whilst the second was in Winston Churchill's office in the Cabinet War Rooms. A large-scale reproduction was built at Cairnryan to enable specialists to test landing techniques.

Men from the COPP wore Kapok uniforms with several pockets to hold the equipment required for their missions, in particular a Colt, a dagger, a compass and a flask of brandy Small rough white board that was attached to the wrist along with a soft lead pencil suitable for writing underwater.
© Copp Heroes Memorial Fund

THE COMBINED OPERATIONS ASSAULT PILOTAGE PARTY

As from 1940, small British teams led reconnaissance raids along the French coast aimed at selecting the most propitious sectors for amphibious operations. Deficient knowledge of the seabed, in particular the presence of natural obstacles (shallows, sandbanks), but also of currents and of the beach itself (sand composition, slope), could lead to disaster. The first missions were led in an empirical manner and equipment was rudimentary. However, 2 years later, Lord Louis Mountbatten created a small special force entirely devoted to this task. The Combined Operations Assault Pilotage Party (COPP) was placed under the orders of Lieutenant Commander Nigel Clogstoun-Willmott. The officer had, in particular, taken part in a surveillance mission off the coast of Rhodes, for a landing operation that never materialised. Ten teams of 2 commandos were formed. Each team was comprised of a combat swimmer and a soldier or officer from the Royal Engineers. They generally began their crossing aboard submarines, to continue towards the coast in canoes. They took geological samples and collected information on the German defences. The COPP organised several missions to Sicily and India throughout the year 1943, before taking part in preparations for Operation Neptune.

Logan Scott-Bowden was transferred to an Engineers unit after operation Gambit. He was awarded the Military Cross. © Copp Heroes Memorial Fund

EISENHOWER'S GAMBLE

Eisenhower scheduled D-Day for the 5th of June, with the possibility of postponing the operation by a few days. The choice of date for the landing depended on a number of parameters: full moon around midnight to facilitate parachute drops and low tide at dawn to enable the landing barges to avoid submerged obstacles. It was decided that men would be landed at dawn and at mid-tide in order to reduce the distance to be covered on the beach, but also so that the sea would cover the first line of underwater obstacles.

Dwight D. Eisenhower.
© Eisenhower Library

To ensure the success of aerial operations, the sky was to be relatively free of low clouds, there was to be no fog and the wind speed was to be under 20 knots in the lower atmosphere and 30 knots near the ground. For the navy, wind was not to be in excess of force 3 on the Beaufort scale and visibility was to be at least 3 nautical miles, i.e. 5km.

RAF Group Captain Stagg's weather service was in charge of collecting and analysing information on the climate so that the SHAEF could launch the operation. All the necessary conditions were reunited early May 1944; however, the barges were as yet in insufficient numbers. The operation was consequently scheduled for the 5th of June, when satisfactory tidal conditions would be

A WELL-KEPT SECRET

Only SHAEF members, a few generals and staff officers were aware of Operation Neptune in all its details. The various echelons of command were gradually informed of the invasion site. Officers were sent to each departure port with the mission of personally handing over sealed "Top Secret" envelopes to each ship's commander. Inside, a second envelope contained a message with the date Operation Neptune was to be launched. Once read, the document was to be burned.

American troops receiving their rations before leaving their transit camp.
© Archives de la Manche

An artillery unit parked in a street and waiting to embark.
© Archives de la Manche

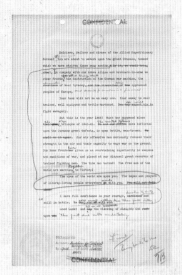
Draft version of the flyer that was to be printed and distributed among the invasion troops.
© Eisenhower Library

found once more. However, on the 2nd of June, Stagg presented Eisenhower with a somewhat pessimistic weather report. He informed that a cold front for Wednesday 7th of June with *"cloudy skies, less than 150 metres of ceiling, force 4 to 5 winds, occasionally 6"* would cross the Channel 24 to 36 hours earlier than previous forecasts. On the 4th, the storm was indeed upon us. Eisenhower decided that very evening to postpone the landing by 24 hours, for a calmer spell was expected the following day. Ships laden with men and material had already left port. Destroyers were sent to meet with ships at the assembly point to the south of the Isle of Wight. The men would need to spend an extra day in the holds of their troop transport ships, tossed by the swell. The next day, Stagg forecast variable weather conditions for the morning of the 6th, with a ceiling between 700 and 900 metres, a westerly wind under force 3 on the beaches and force 4 off shore, and good visibility that should remain till the afternoon.

Eisenhower knew he could wait no longer. Any further postponement would be catastrophic. The moon and tide conditions would not be reunited again for 2 weeks. The assault troops were perfectly familiar with their objective and the secret could not be kept for long if they returned to dry land. Opinions among SHAEF officers were divided. Ike finally decided to risk all.

IN CASE OF FAILURE LETTER

"Our landings in the Cherbourg-Havre are a have failed to gain a satisfactory foothold and I have withdrawn the troops. My decision to attack at this time and place was based upon the best information available. The troops, the air and the Navy did all that bravery and devotion to duty could do. If any blame of fault attaches to the attempt, it is mine alone. 5th June."

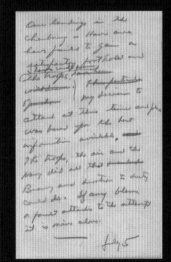

The message written by the SHAEF commander to be broadcast only in the case of failure. © Eisenhower Library

EMBARKATION

The 34,000 men and 3,300 vehicles from Force O had been sent to their assembly points during the first fortnight in May. The men, who knew nothing of their final destination, were stationed in tented camps surrounded with barbed wire and under strict surveillance. They were to have no contact whatsoever with the outside world to avoid any information leak. The Military Police kept a watchful eye. The men were issued with their equipment. Over the last days of May, all units converged at the embarkation ports in Portland, Weymouth and Poole. Seven troop transport vessels, 8 LSIs, 24 LSTs, 33 LCIs, 36 LCMs, 147 LCTs and 33 other vessels awaited them. Over 3 days, Port of Embarkation specialists assembled, directed and loaded vehicles and their crews on board the ships. Troops boarded 2 days before the landing operation.

Transportation Corps armband and insignia.
© VD Collection

Heavily laden Rangers in the tight hull of an LCA.
© USCMH

GIs leaving an LCVP to board their transport ship.
© USCMH

US Navy overall.
© Mémorial de Caen

Embarking vehicles in the port of Brixham. © USCMH

Transportation Corps helmet.
© P. Caje Collection

U.S. NAVY

A Coast Guards crew off Omaha Beach.
They are wearing their skull and crossbones
helmets. © USCG

CHAPTER 3

AT DAWN

A MISLED GERMAN COMMAND

The German military chiefs knew that the invasion was imminent, but the weather forecasts they had at their disposal led them to believe that the enemy would make no attempt over the next fortnight. No aerial reconnaissance mission had been led over the ports on the south English coast due to bad weather. In contrast with the Allied weather department, experts from the *Luftwaffe* had forecast no improvement for the early days of June. And the Allies had never launched an amphibious operation with weather conditions being perfect.

Die Wehrmacht newspapers issued in May 1944. The German army was keen to convince that it was finally ready to drive the Allies back westwards.
© VD Collection

On the 5th of June, the *Kriegsmarine* decided not to send out its motor torpedo boats and minelayers from the ports of Le Havre and Cherbourg. Convinced that the Allies would make no attempt whatsoever, several high-ranking military officers and unit commanders had even left their positions. A *Kriegspiel*, reuniting several unit commanders, was to be held in Rennes on the morning of the 6th of June. The proposed theme was premonitory: an enemy landing in the Cotentin peninsula, preceded by airborne troop drops. Kraiss and Richter had stayed at their positions. Manoeuvres were planned for the days that followed.

LES SANGLOTS LONGS DES VIOLONS DE L'AUTOMNE...

The broadcast by the BBC, after the French-speaking evening news, of 2 lines from a poem by Verlaine entitled *Chanson d'automne*, were aimed at informing the French Resistance of the launch of the Allied landing operation. The first line was to be broadcast on the 1st or the 15th of the month during which the operation would take place. The second would indicate that the landings were within 48 hours and would be the order to implement planned sabotage operations (railway lines, pylons, roads, bridges...) in order to paralyse German army communication and movement.

The *Abwehr* (the German intelligence department), which had infiltrated several Resistance networks, was aware of the meaning of the 2 messages. The first line of the poem was picked up on the 1st of June by the department, located in Tourcoing, in charge of permanently listening to the British radio station. The information was immediately forwarded to *Oberst* Helmut Meyer, the intelligence officer from the military staff of the *15. Armee*. The news was not taken seriously. At 9.15pm on the evening of the 5th of June, over a period of 16 minutes, a total of 210 messages informed the French Resistance of the imminent armed action. The second line inspired by the poem, *bercent mon coeur d'une langueur monotone*, drew Meyer's attention. He immediately notified *Generaloberst* von Salmuth, who put his troops on maximum alert, simultaneously informing the headquarters of *Heeresgruppe B* in La Roche-Guyon, followed by the commander-in-chief for the West, *Generalfeldmarschall* von Rundstedt. However, the *7. Armee* in charge of defending the Normandy coast never received the information.

A German radio operator.

CROSSING THE CHANNEL

The 700 vessels that comprised Force O left their respective ports on the 4th of June at different times and headed for the assembly point located to the south-west of the Isle of Wight, codenamed Piccadilly Circus. The armada was then divided into 9 convoys and set off southwards. Battleships, cruisers, destroyers, tugboats, tankers, hospital ships and auxiliary ships were scattered over 30 kilometres of sea line. Sixteen troop transport ships and 10 Landing Ship Tanks were deployed to transport the 10,000 men that were to land on Omaha. Half of them were British ships. In close files, they sailed the 360 metre-wide channels cleared by British and Canadian minesweepers. Lit acoustic buoys were laid in order to mark out the channels. The work done by the minesweepers

An LCI convoy crossing the English Channel. © NARA

A Coast Guards launch keeping watch over the barges. © NARA

FORCE O

Commander:
Rear-Admiral John Hall

Flagship
USS Ancon (AGC-4)

Ships transporting the 16th Infantry Regiment
USS Samuel Chase (APA-26)
USS Henrico (APA-45)
HMS Empire Anvil (LSI(L))

Ship transporting the 18th Infantry Regiment
USS Anne Arundel (AP-76)

Ships transporting the 116th Infantry Regiment
LSI(L) HMS Empire Javelin
USS Thomas Jefferson (APA-30)
USS Charles Carroll (APA-28)

Ships transporting the 2nd Rangers
LSI(S) HMS Prince Charles
HMS Ben Machree
HMS Amsterdam

Ships transporting the 5th Rangers
HMS Prince Leopold
HMS Prince Baudouin
HMS Princess Maud

Ships transporting several units
USS Dorothea Dix (AP-67)
USS Thurston (AP-77)
USS Oceanway
LST 6, 310, 314, 315, 316, 317, 357, 374, 375, 376

A STRANGE FOREBODING.

At dusk, on the 5th of June, Master Sergeant John Dean and Private Louis Milam were chatting on the deck of *USS Thomas Jefferson*. The two men, who were friends since high school, both belonged to the 116th Infantry Division's Company F. Just like many other soldiers, they were speculating as to their chances of surviving the terrible battle that awaited them. Death haunted their thoughts over long hours. John had a strange foreboding. He silently removed his ring, took out his wallet and asked his friend if he could take them to give them back to his mother when he returned back home. Louis refused, but John insisted, so his friend finally accepted and tucked them away in his pocket. The following morning, on Omaha, a German shell exploded in the midst of the company. Sergeant Dean was killed instantly.

Enamelled 116th Infantry Regiment insignia.

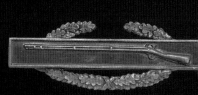

Insignia.

was vital for success. Thankfully, the 8km-deep minefield that was supposed to forbid any access by Allied ships to the French coast was almost empty.

The ships needed to sail essentially by daylight, for nights are short at that time of year. The *Luftwaffe* planes and the *Kriegsmarine S-Boote* (motor torpedo boat) flotillas could appear at any time. The tragedy of the 28th of April was still fresh in many memories. In the case of shipwreck, hundreds of men could be lost. Their chances of survival were very slim. The Channel waters are so cold that any castaways could only remain conscious for around fifteen minutes.

Opération *Neptune*.

THE EVE OF BATTLE

For the officers, soldiers and sailors, the last hours spent aboard their vessels were quite singular. The men counted the ships and gazed at the planes that flew above them.

On the ships' decks, some men joked, chatted or sang, whilst others remained solemn and silent. Chaplains gave religious services on the upper decks and tried to comfort the men, in the knowledge that many of them were living their last hours. In dormitories, a few managed to sleep the sleep of the just, whilst others scoured magazines or the conversation booklets they had been issued with prior to boarding, or gambled their pay or their invasion money at poker or dice. Some soldiers isolated themselves to write a last letter to their parents, their fiancée or their wife. The most unperturbed among them chased their worries by gambling their pay at dice or on improvised card tables. In principal, they had all they needed... Yet, soldiers were not all housed in the same boat, so to speak. Whilst large troop transport ships

Information leaflet issued to the Marine Corps on life aboard troop transport ships. Found in Normandy.
© VD Collection

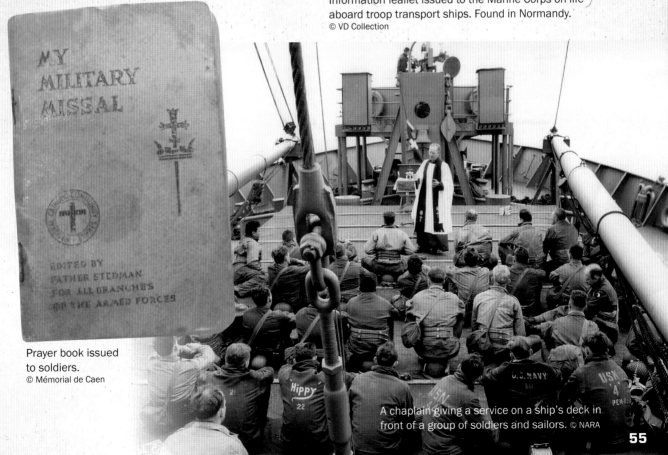

Prayer book issued to soldiers.
© Mémorial de Caen

A chaplain giving a service on a ship's deck in front of a group of soldiers and sailors. © NARA

Men from the 1st US Infantry Division on a ship's deck. The presence of Springfield M1907 rifles suggests they are part of a support unit. © US Navy

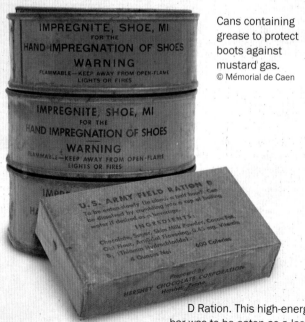

Cans containing grease to protect boots against mustard gas. © Mémorial de Caen

D Ration. This high-energy chocolate bar was to be eaten as a last resort and upon orders. © VD Collection

offered relative comfort, the same could not be said of the Landing Craft Tank and Landing Craft Infantry, that the storm readily tossed about in all directions.

Action stations were sounded a few hours late. The Normandy coast was within sight...

The DCA, on the alert, had received orders to shoot down any plane that was not painted with black and white invasion stripes. P-38 Lightning fighter planes, easily recognisable thanks to their distinctive twin booms, were chosen to avoid them being confused with *Luftwaffe* aircraft.

Lines of LCVPs on their way to the beach. *USS Augusta* can be seen in the background. © NARA

TRANSHIPMENT

It was 2 o'clock in the morning when the first ships from the Western Task Force came within sight of the Normandy coast. Force O's flagship, *USS Ancon*, cast anchor 20km off the coast. It was soon joined by the cruiser *USS Augusta*, the Western Task Force 122's flagship, commanded by Rear-Admiral Alan Kirk. Major General Omar Bradley was also on board.

Each ship took up its planned position, according to a well-orchestrated ballet. The troop transport ships anchored 18km from the coast, out of the coastal batteries' range. Minesweepers cleared the access channels for the landing barges, whereas bombing force ships headed for their firing sector. The destroyers continued to within 4,500 metres of the beach to lay an artificial smoke screen in order to conceal the armada from the enemy gaze.

As on Utah, H-Hour had been scheduled at 6.30am. To ensure the success of the operation, the beach was divided into 4 sectors: Charlie, Dog, Easy and Fox, which were in turn split into 2 or 3 sub-sections designated by means of a colour.

An LCVP moving away from *USS Samuel Chase* (APA-26) with its Assault Boat Team. © Magnum

TESTIMONY

"At around 4am, on the 6th of June 1944, we were wakened by a radio message by General Eisenhower. He thanked us and told us we were going to take part in the invasion of Normandy, which had begun by night drops of parachutists and troops from gliders."

Private Allen Levin, 29th US Infantry Division, 115th Regiment, Company C.

THE ASSAULT BOAT TEAMS

The combat groups that were boarded onto barges needed to be capable of fulfilling their mission independently of other troops. Each team was comprised of an officer, a non-commissioned officer, 5 fusiliers (Rifle Team), 2 teams of machine gunners equipped with FM Bars (Bar Team), a 4-man breach team equipped with wire cutters and Bangalore torpedoes (Wire Cutting Team), four 60mm mortar servers (Mortar Team), 2 men equipped with a flamethrower (Flamethrower Team) and one demolition team of 5 sappers (Demolition Team). The composition of the Support Boat Teams was virtually identical. The 60mm mortar and FM Bar were replaced by one 81mm mortar and calibre 30 machine guns. These figures remain theoretical for the barges were overloaded with command unit and liaison staff and with gunners in charge of controlling artillery fire.

Transhipment of the first assault troops began at 2.30am. The LCAs and LCVPs were shifted from their davits and set to sea. The operation took over an hour. The heavily laden infantrymen assembled on their ships' decks as officers made their ultimate roll call. The soldiers grasped as best they could the rope nets and ladders that hung down the flanks of the ships before squeezing inside the cramped barges. The 1.5 to 2 metre swell generated by the 4 to 5 Beaufort scale north-westerly winds complicated the manoeuvre.

The Coast Guard seamen transhipped equipment and helped the overladen GIs to reach their flat-bottomed barges in the dark of the night. The men needed to wait for the right moment to board the barges that the swell incessantly surged up and down the planking. Some men found themselves squashed between the two hulls on their way down. Once on board, they were meticulously positioned depending on their speciality and their weapons.

Once the operation was complete, the barges moved off and turned round the troop transport ships pending the end of transhipment. At around 4.30am, the barges formed columns which began their long procession towards the start line.

Infantrymen equipped with their assault jackets being transferred to LCVPs. © NARA

Sergeant Felix Branham from the 116th Infantry Regiment's Company K was armed with an M1 rifle and took with him 286 cartridges, 10 grenades, 10kg of TNT, half a dozen detonators, K-rations for 2 days and 3 D-rations.

THE AMPHIBIOUS SCOUTS AND RAIDERS

In 1943, the US Navy created a small unit specialising in nocturnal amphibious raids. The Scouts and Raiders were also capable of marking out the beaches and guiding the assault forces. They had earned themselves a solid reputation in the Mediterranean. Their chief, Lieutenant Phil Bucklew, a former American football player, was awarded the Navy Cross and the Silver Star for his action in Sicily and Salerno. The S&R joined Task Force 122 in England in December 1943. A month later, Bucklew and another officer, Grant Andreasen, were sent on a nocturnal mission on what was to become Omaha Beach, in order to take samples of sand and to study currents. A few weeks later, British commandos took them back there aboard kayaks. After swimming to the beach, they monitored and timed the German patrols for several hours.

On the 6th of June, 9 Landing Craft Controls, with the Scouts and Raiders on board, lined up the barges on their start line. Landing Craft Support (LCS) vessels guided the lines of barges as far as the beach. The LCSs boasted an armoured steering compartment and powerful weapons, hence enabling them to cover the first waves of assault.

The Scouts & Raiders in training at Fort Pierce in Florida. Their training programme was intense: walking, swimming, obstacle courses, shooting, close combat, transmission, signal and weaponry courses. © Navy Seal Museum

USM3 Trench Knife
manufactured by Boker.
© VD Collection

NAVAL BOMBARDMENT

The navy and the air force had been entrusted with the mission of bombarding the German coastal defences and of reducing them to silence before the arrival of the first waves of assault. The bombardment, conducted immediately before dawn, only lasted thirty minutes. Prior to the attack, a total of 60 targets had been meticulously identified. Bombardment Group C's battleships and cruisers were 16.5km off the coast and the destroyers were at less than 5km.

The naval artillery came into action at 5.40am, bombarding the German fortified positions established along the coast prior to the landing of any troops. To the west of Omaha, the venerable cruiser *Texas*, in service since 1914, acted as the flagship. Its ten 355mm artillery pieces pounded Pointe du Hoc, whilst its 127mm guns bombed the D-1 exit road level with the village of Vierville.

USS Arkansas, anchored to the east, dealt with the locality referred to as Les Moulins and attacked the Longues-sur-Mer artillery battery. The cruiser

Fragment of a naval shell belt found on the heights above Omaha Beach.

HMS Glasgow bombarded Pointe du Hoc, whilst the other 3 cruisers attacked Port-en-Bessin, paying particular attention to the *Kriegsmarine* artillery barges berthed in the harbour. The destroyers in turn dealt with the fortified positions located on the heights.

The four 152mm triple turrets aboard the cruiser *HMS Glasgow* bombarded the western sector of Omaha Beach.

A LONG-DISTANCE DUEL

Shortly after 5.30am, the cruisers *Georges Leygues, Montcalm* and *USS Arkansas* bombed the Longues-sur-Mer artillery battery which, consequently, struck back. The German shells straddled the cruiser, but retaliation from French ships and the destroyers *USS Doyle* and *Emmons* obliged the *Kriegsmarine* gunners to turn their target towards the Gold Beach sector. The 152mm guns then hit *HMS Bulolo,* which was transporting the British XXX Corps' headquarters. The ship headed further out to sea for protection. The intervention by the cruiser *HMS Ajax* obliged the Germans to cease fire at around 6.20am. Yet, 20 minutes later, their guns began to fire once more on the American troops as they landed on Omaha Beach. The *Ajax* and the cruiser *HMS Argonaut* joined forces to silence them. Three of the four 152mm artillery pieces were put out of action. The

The battleship *USS Arkansas*, launched in 1911, opened fire at 5.52 am. Its 305mm guns fired on the Longues-sur-Mer artillery battery. © US Navy

last gun continued to fire till 5pm. On the 7th of June, the garrison's 184 demoralised soldiers surrendered to the British troops.

"There would be a flash like a blast furnace from the 14-inch guns of the Texas, that would lick far out from the ship. Then the yellow-brown smoke would cloud out and, with the smoke still rolling, the concussion and the report would hit us, jarring the men's helmets. It struck your near ear like a punch with a heavy, dry glove. Then up on the green rise of a hill that now showed clearly as we moved in would spout two tall black fountains of earth and smoke [...]"

Ernest Hemingway.

To the rear, the LCTs served as floating batteries. The Sherman M4 tanks and self-propelled Priest M7 howitzers fired above the barge landing ramps. However, the heavy swell, poor visibility and nervousness of the gunners rendered their fire inaccurate. The Allied guns suddenly became silent at 6.27am. Although formidable, naval fire was far too long and barely grazed the German defences.

A support force, comprised of 5 Landing Craft (Gun) and 12 Landing Craft Tank (Rocket) entered the scene a few minutes before the first barges reached the beach. This concentrated fire, capable of saturating a 700 metre-wide by 220 metre-deep zone was as spectacular to the defenders as it was to the assailants; however, its efficacy was virtually non-existent because of the swell and the impossibility for crews to aim without simultaneously manoeuvring ships. Almost all the rockets they fired exploded in the surf.

An LCT(R) entered into action a few minutes before the first wave of assault. © Rights reserved

B-24 Liberator
bomber. © USAF

FOR A FEW SECONDS

Six minutes later, a deafening roar resounded. Four hundred and forty B-24 Liberator bombers from the 8th USAAF 2nd Bombardment Division, flying at high altitude, opened their holds to drop their deadly cargo on the German positions. Each of the 12 fortified zones was bombarded by 36 planes, divided into 6 waves. The 50kg bombs were equipped with instantaneous fuses that made them explode as soon as they hit the ground. Crews were not accustomed to working so early in the morning.

The dim light of dawn and the heavy clouds obliged bombers to fire at random. They were to report back to the "Mickey" H2X radar that equipped the 20 reconnaissance planes. This state-of-the art equipment guided plane formations towards their targets. Their firing range was minimal. A few seconds too early, and their bombs would hit the first wave of assault which had begun its approach. A few seconds too late, and their targets would be missed.

MISSION IMPOSSIBLE

The use of strategic aviation above Omaha was a subject of much debate within both the US Army and the US Navy. Since 1942, American crews had been continuously bombarding Germany. Daytime strikes and the use of Norden sights had not enabled the expected level of accuracy to be attained. Furthermore, many military chiefs had doubts as to the efficacy of heavy bombers in supporting ground troops. It was a delicate operation. Planes flying at high altitude needed to drop their bombs into a tiny target zone and with no visibility. They also needed to avoid hitting the flotillas of barges that were barely 3km from their targets. And they were to avoid the beaches, for the craters their bombs would leave were likely to jeopardise the landing of vehicles.

The bombers strictly abided by the orders they had been given during their briefing, dropping their bombs after a 20 to 30 second delay to ensure they spared the barges. Hundreds of projectiles flooded out of their holds like waterfalls, before disappearing from sight amidst the clouds. A total of 1,285 tonnes of bombs exploded 5km inland, on either side of the RN13 main road. A few artillery positions were hit. Several civilians were killed, as was a quantity of livestock. The aviation suffered no losses. The bomber crews returned to their base, convinced that they had accomplished their mission to perfection.

The hills that overlook the beach were obscured by clouds of smoke and dust.
© US Navy

AMPHIBIOUS TANKS

Sixty-eight tanks belonging to the 741st and 743rd Tank Battalions were to arrive a few minutes before the assault infantry. The B and C Companies of each unit were equipped with Sherman Duplex Drives, amphibious tanks that could float and move about in water. They had 2 propellers, a deck and a watertight canvas skirt that was stiffened by rubber tubes, inflated with compressed air, and by metal frames. Sixteen Landing Craft Tanks (LCT) were in charge of putting them to sea. However, the fates of the 2 armoured forces were quite different.

At 5.30am (H-60), the 8 LCTs that were transporting 2 companies from the 741st Tank Battalion were 5.4km from Omaha Beach, opposite the Fox Green and Easy Red sectors. Their mission was to support the 16th RCT. The force 4 wind and the swell were of concern to both companies' commanders, Captain Thornton and Captain Young, for they had never been faced with any such situation during training manoeuvres in England. Aware of the major role their tanks would play during the battle, they took the risk of putting them to sea, despite warnings from Lieutenant Barry, the flotilla's commander.

The 34-tonne monsters headed for their ramps and plunged into the murky Channel waters. A few seconds later, the waves submerged the 30cm of the skirts' freeboard, twisting the frames and sending the tanks to the depths. The other armoured vehicles put to sea met with the same fate. Torrents of icy water flooded into the access hatches that had been left open. The men, equipped with breathing devices, waited till the tanks were full of water before extricating themselves from the steel carcasses and heading for the surface. The castaways grasped onto the lifeboats as they awaited the Coast Guard cutters, in water at 14°C, under the helpless gaze of the occupants of nearby assault barges. The 741st had just lost 27 tanks and 33 of its 135 men.

Sherman M4A3 Duplex Drive tank equipped with its removable canvas floatation screen which kept it above water. Once landed, the propellers and the screen were removed.

This DD tank has just left its LCT and is heading for the waters. This rare scene, filmed during an exercise in England, perfectly illustrates how dangerous the operation was. For safety reasons, the British crew has remained outside. © DR

Out at sea, off Vierville, Lieutenant Commander Rockwell and Captain Elder from the 743rd Tank Battalion, decided not to put their tanks to sea, convinced they would sink as soon as they hit the water. The 8 LCTs manoeuvred to perfection and advanced in line towards the beach. LCT 607 hit a mine. All its crew members were killed or wounded in the explosion. Four tanks were lost.

Lieutenant Bucklew from the Scouts and Raiders was in charge of guiding the LCTs that transported the 741st Battalion's DD tanks. This highly experienced officer very quickly grasped that the conditions were too bad to put the armoured vehicles to sea. He tried to reach the chief of the convoy by radio; however, his message was ignored.

TESTIMONY

Aboard his LCT 600, Sergeant Paul Ragan, who was in the second tank, saw a sailor lower the yellow pennant, which was the sign of imminent departure. The ramp lowered and the lead vehicle headed for the waters, to sink in just a few seconds. At that very instant, a nearby explosion shook the ship. The tanks slid along the deck and concertinaed, ripping up the floatation skirts. The crew of the first tank was rescued. The LCT 600's 3 DD tanks were landed on the beach to reach their planned sector. Very quickly, one of them was destroyed and the two others headed off to support the infantry and the engineers for 7 long hours.

A castaway being rescued by the crew of a Coast Guards speed boat. © US Navy

The barges lowered their ramps at 6.40am (H+10). The Sherman DDs, their skirts lowered, advanced slowly through the waves and strove to cut a path through the obstacles.

Sixteen Royal Navy LCT(A)s, transporting the A Companies of 2 battalions were grounded on the beach a few minutes of each other. The Shermans were equipped with large sheet metal exhaust chimneys on their rear decks in order to enable them to move in water without drowning the engine. A total of 48 tanks were deployed; however, by 7 in the morning, 14 of them had already been destroyed or abandoned due to damage. The others were stuck on the beach. They covered the infantry and tried to muzzle the German antitank guns, in particular the formidable 88 mm pieces on *WN 61* and *WN 72*.

MISSING IN ACTION

This bronze tank propeller, produced in February 1944, belonged to one of the 741st Tank Battalion's 27 Sherman Duplex Drive tanks that sunk 6km off Omaha Beach. The tank was discovered by a Norman diver in the 1980s. The US Navy quickly sent a Navy Seals team to the site in order to recover the bodies of the crew, lost since 1944. Due to the force of the water that gushed through the hatches, the men had apparently found themselves blocked inside the tank and had drowned. The Americans thanked the tank's discoverer by offering him one of its 2 propellers.

DD tank propeller.
© Aiolfi & Partners

PIERCED LCVP RAMP

Thanks to firing plans it had established over the previous months and to its advanced observers, the German artillery proved to be of deadly accuracy. The German mortars, *Nebelwerfer* and howitzers brought death and destruction. On Omaha Beach, on the 6th of June, a total of 22 LCVPs, 4 LCTs and 2 LCIs were destroyed by obstacles and the artillery.

This LCVP ramp was torn apart by 2 projectiles. The first tore up the steel ramp before it was opened and the second once it was lowered. The crew and the assault troop on board unquestionably suffered heavy losses.

© Omaha Beach Museum

An LCVP transporting a 1st US Infantry Division Team Assault Company towards Omaha. The men are crouching in the bottom of the barge to protect themselves from the sea spray and from enemy fire. The officer, who can be recognised thanks to the white horizontal band on the back of his helmet, is in the foreground. © NARA

CHAPTER 4

THE FIRST WAVE

THE ASSAULT

The 48 LCA and LCVP barges transporting the 1,450 men that comprised the first wave of assault made their way to the coast. Their pilots, often young and inexperienced, did their best to keep these "matchboxes" going in the right direction. The heavy swell, current and poor visibility already made their task an extremely dangerous one. The obstacles and the intensity of enemy fire were to make it even more complex, and deadly.

Inside the barges, fear and stress gradually increased as the fateful hour approached. The infantrymen, cramped and stiffened by the cold,

were soaked by the huge waves that came crashing down on them. Many fell victim to sea sickness. The Dramamine tablets they had been given before boarding were of no effect. Their heavy helmets were given a new purpose that the army had surely never planned for. The men also had to use them to empty out water from some barges, the pumps proving insufficient. Ten barges sank, covering the seas with men and their equipment. Then they all stopped at around 400m from the shoreline.

The German defences entered the scene as soon as their landing ramps were lowered. Bursts of

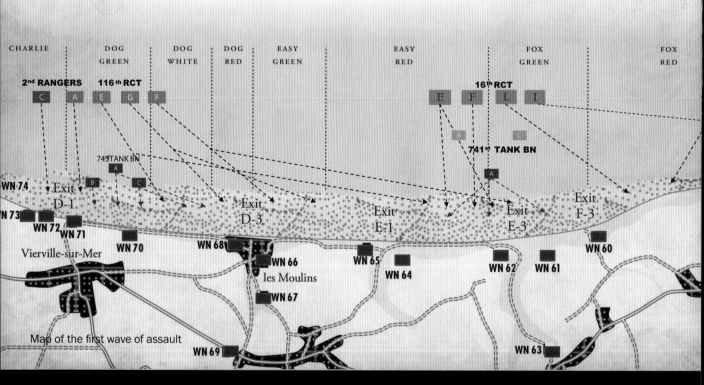

Map of the first wave of assault

British sailors and an officer from the Big Red One observing the coast from aboard an LCA. © Mémorial de Caen.

An infantry assault troop advancing in the water. On the beach, men from the first wave of assault are lying down behind the obstacles along the pebbled embankment. © NARA

TESTIMONY

"The water was deep and the only thing to do was to plunge into it. All the time I was in the water, bullets hit the waves, right under my nose and all around me. I mulled over all the sins I had committed during my short life and I think I have never prayed so intensely... On the shore, the beach was studded with obstacles – we were landing at low tide... There was a dune, and it was the only sheltered place since we'd left the boat. The only thing to do was to cross the beach under enemy fire and to take refuge there, but, for a while, that was impossible. The beach was under German machine gun crossfire, sweeping across from the fortifications located on the heights. I advanced around thirty yards and threw myself to the ground: bullets were coming from everywhere... When I hit the sand, a bullet pierced through my bag, my radio and my antenna. At another moment, a shell exploded just ten feet away from me. I was stunned for a few seconds by the blow. I finally managed to reach the seafront... Then I turned round to see how my section was trying to make it through: it was a horrible sight... Men were dying all around me. The wounded couldn't move and began to drown in the rising tide. And since the landing barges were on fire, they had no place for shelter... eighty percent of our weapons - including mine - had been put out of action by the sand and the salty water."

Robert Hutch, 1st US Infantry Division, 16th RCT

machine gunfire swept through the inside of the barges, killing the first rows outright. Hailstorms of shells and mortar projectiles beat down on the American infantrymen. They were taken by surprise by the sheer intensity of enemy fire, totally unaware that the prior bombardment had failed. They advanced, totally exposed, in 50cm of water. Laden with their equipment, they ran to take shelter behind the first line of obstacles. Others lay down in the shallow waters, letting the tide sweep them to shore, to avoid drawing the attention of the German gunners. Very quickly, panic and confusion were rife. The dazed troops could not recognise the terrain they had studied so often back in England. Over the first hour, the majority of units suffered 30% losses.

A German antitank gun entering into action. © Bundesarchiv

AMPHIBIOUS TROOP EQUIPMENT

The men belonging to assault formations took with them gas masks in black watertight bags, haversacks and ammunition belts, a range of tools, Bangalore torpedoes and M1A1 bazookas. Some companies were equipped with ladders for them to climb up antitank ditches. Demolition team members carried 7kg handheld charges and 5.4kg charges mounted on wooden stakes. In their haversacks, they also had General Purpose consumables, demolition equipment and explosives. Rifles, pistols and automatic weapons were swathed in Pliofilm covers. All men were issued with gas detection paper armbands. Their uniforms were generally soaked with a sticky and nauseating antigas agent. Their laced boots were polished with special grease. Each man was provided with a watertight pouch containing an first aid dressing, a tourniquet and a dose of morphine. He was also given a 250g stick of explosives with an igniter so that he could blow up a hole in the sand to shelter from enemy fire.

Shell case for nurses
Out in the field, units used the equipment they deemed best to ensure they accomplish their mission. They invented, recovered and improvised. Hence, this cardboard 155mm shell case has been transformed into a first aid box thanks to its appropriate capacity and its watertightness. Red crosses have been stencilled onto it to facilitate the identification of its contents. The list of these contents is written on the plaster that closes the case.

© Big Red One Museum

Assault Jacket
The GIs wore cotton canvas Assault Jackets that had been specially designed for amphibious operations. Their wide pockets could carry ammunition, food supplies and individual equipment. Their straps enabled the jacket to be quickly unfastened to avoid drowning. In truth, the garment proved to be heavy, uncomfortable and too hot. Many soldiers quickly got rid of them so they could advance more quickly.

© F. Potin Collection

© Aiolfi & Partners

Bangalore torpedo

The M1A1 torpedo was used by the US Army to open wide breaches in barbed wire fence networks. The torpedo consisted of several steel tubes that were 1.5m in length and 5cm in diameter and contained 38.5kg of TNT. The men in charge of installing them had to push the torpedo under the barbed wire whilst assembling the tubes together before triggering the device from a distance using an electric detonator. The use of this type of torpedo could prove deadly for it took place under enemy fire and the area around barbed wire networks was often mined.

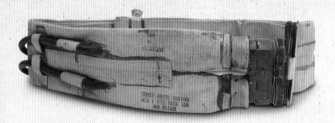

© VD Collection

© VD Collection

Life Preserver Belt M1926

All soldiers were issued with an M-1926 lifebelt. Its rubber canvas tubes could be automatically inflated using small carbon dioxide bottles or by blowing into them. This belt could prove dangerous if worn round the waist. Men, laden with the weight of their kit bags, toppled forwards and drowned. In order to reduce this risk, experienced GIs used string to keep their belts at chest level.

Pliofilm cover

These transparent or green-died vinyl covers, used to protect firearms from the sand and seawater, were deemed unpractical. Wrapped-up rifles could not be carried on the shoulder during barge transport. Not being able to use one's weapon before reaching the beach also proved to be a drawback. Many soldiers used condoms to seal the barrel. A great number of firearms were lost in the sea, whilst others were rendered unfit for use, the mechanism jammed by the sand.

Watertight radio bag

Transmission is of major importance during military operations and at all levels of command. As such, on the 6th of June 1944, radio equipment was enclosed within specially designed rubber canvas bags. This bag, which could hold an SCR-300 radio, was found near the town of Coutances, which was liberated late July by the 1st US Infantry Division and the 3rd Armored Division.

© VD Collection

M-5 Assault Gas Mask

A specific gas mask was issued to assault troops. It was relatively compact thanks to the position of its filter cartridge on the left side. Its black transport cover was totally watertight. Soldiers used the bag as a haversack during the Normandy campaign.

© VD Collection

A *Weintraub* war correspondent taking a series of photographs of GIs from an ESB helping troops whose barge has sunk. The wounded are being taken care of. Several bodies are lying near the lifebelts. © NARA

GAP ASSAULT TEAMS

Gap Assault Teams belonging to the 146th and the 299th Engineer Combat Battalions were in charge of opening 16 corridors, each of a width of fifty metres. They were to destroy any obstacles before they were covered by the high tide and to mark out breaches. They were assisted by the US Navy's Naval Combat Demolition Unit Teams (NCDU). These specialists dealt with underwater obstacles. Sixteen Tankdozers, Sherman tanks equipped with bulldozer blades, were supposed to fill the holes made by shells and the antitank ditches, and to clear any wrecks.

Lieutenant Colonel O'Neill's Special Engineer Task Force was, in theory, to land at H+3; however, the Landing Craft Mechanized (LCM) barges arrived 15 minutes after the infantry. Several barges drifted excessively eastwards. Five of them reached their intended destinations. Most of the heavy equipment was lost. The Germans concentrated their fire on men laden with equipment and on their inflatable dinghies filled with explosives. Several LCMs were hit by the artillery. Only 6 Tankdozers reached the beach. Very soon, 3 of them were destroyed by German antitank guns.

The men were struggling to accomplish their mission due to the sheer intensity of enemy fire and the infantrymen cramped behind the obstacles for shelter. Lieutenant Colonel Carl J. Isley, commander of the 146th Engineer Combat Battalion, realised the difficulty his men were in and landed on the beach to reorganise his teams. He stayed by his sappers through the most crucial moments of the battle. A piece of shrapnel pierced through his heavy helmet, ripping his underhelmet

An Engineer's canvas haversack and demolition equipment. His Denny and his regimental number have been stencilled onto the flap and the strap. © VD Collection

AHEAD OF SCHEDULE

The barge transporting Second Lieutenant Phil Wood's Team 14 reached the Easy Red sector 5 minutes before the infantry and tanks. Barely had they landed when a shell hit their barge, killing all the men who were still on board. Wood and the rest of his team abandoned their explosive-laden dinghy to avoid the same fate. Without cover, enemy fire put half of Team 14 out of action in just a few minutes.

cap, but Isley was miraculously unscathed. He grabbed his helmet, without dwelling on what had just happened and he continued his mission.

The sappers and NCDUs also continued under enemy fire and despite their losses. They set explosive charges before installing traction igniters and unrolling the 30 metre-long Primacord detonating cord. Pencil detonators that were to be placed in water were protected with condoms. Once connected to each other, the explosive charges were linked to a detonator. All fit and wounded men were to be moved away from the nearby area before

ignition. Several teams saw their work reduced to smithereens after detonating cords were cut by barges or tanks as they made their way across the beach.

Demolition teams successfully opened six 50 metre breaches. Two of them were in the Dog sector and the 4 others on Easy Red. Three further breaches were partially opened. White pennants were hoisted onto poles to guide tank drivers through feasible corridors. Once they had accomplished their task, the sappers joined the assault troops and waited for the tide to go out before continuing their work.

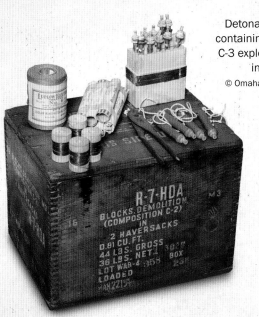

Detonators and case containing 16 sticks of C-3 explosives packed in canvas bags.
© Omaha Beach Memorial Museum

First model satchel bag used to transport explosive charges.
© Big Red One Museum

VIERVILLE

The 7 LCAs that were transporting the 116th RCT's Company A advanced with difficulty, constantly taking in water from above the bow. Two barges sunk. The others grounded on the Dog Green sand banks opposite Vierville at 6.30am. Barely had their landing ramps been lowered when the bullets from light weapons and machine guns swept across the sand and the water then the ramps and the decks of the LCAs. During training, the men had been taught to leave their vessels spreading out in fan formations. One column would thrust forward in the centre, whilst the other 2 would do the same on either side. However, the men were mowed down before even leaving their barges. Some of them hoped their fellow soldiers in front would help them escape death, but the bullets pierced straight through their bodies. Staying on the beach signified certain death. They needed to climb over bodies and jump off their barges whilst avoiding the areas that were riddled by enemy fire. The men found themselves in 1.5 metre-deep water, carrying their weapons above their heads. The waves and the weight of their pack rendered their progression extremely difficult.

Some men pressed their bodies against the obstacles, others crawled across the sand before returning to the water for protection. Amidst the floating bodies, survivors tried to conceal themselves in the waves, feigning death and letting themselves float freely. Two lonely tanks fired on enemy bunkers, whilst clusters of infantrymen hurried inland to protect themselves against the projectiles.

TESTIMONY

"Fire, Wegner, fire!" Lang yelled to me. I was paralysed; I had seen all those men in khaki uniforms wading their way through the water towards the sand. They looked defenceless in the midst of the beach. Lang took the stock of his pistol and violently hit my helmet with it. The metallic sound roused me and I pressed the trigger. The MG rumbled, sending bullets into the men who were running across the beach. I saw some of them fall; I knew I had hit them. The bullets raked the sand from top to bottom. A young man from Hanover had just killed several men. My mind rationalised it all, this was war. But even so, it left a bitter taste. The time had come to stop talking, and simply to survive."

Private Wegner, 3. *Kompanie, I./914. Infanterie Regiment, 352. ID WN72*

The fearsome Pak 43 gun - photographed after the battle. © NARA

THE STEVENS BROTHERS

Roy and Ray (the younger by 20 minutes) were twins from a family of 14 siblings who grew up in Virginia in the midst of the Great Depression. The two brothers, who were inseparable, abandoned their studies and bought a small farm to help their family before joining the National Guard. In 1942, they landed in Great Britain with the rest of the 29th US Infantry Division. Promoted to the grade of Sergeant, the two brothers shared the same barracks and each trained his own platoon from the 116th Infantry Regiment's Company A. On the morning of the 6th of June, they shook hands and agreed to meet up at a crossroads at Vierville-sur-Mer. Barge n°4 in which Roy was travelling sunk after violently hitting an obstacle. The weight of his pack dragged Roy to the depths; however, he was saved from drowning by one of his men who cut the straps of his kit bag. The barge's survivors were recovered after 2 hours and were repatriated to England. With no news of Ray, Roy then landed once more on Omaha Beach 3 days later. A nurse informed him that his brother had been seriously wounded by machine gunfire on the 6th of June and that he had died on the beach. Sergeant Roy Stevens found his brother's grave 7 days later thanks to the military ID tag hanging on one of the wooden crosses in Omaha's temporary cemetery. He could not find the strength to announce the terrible news to his family.

Photograph of Roy Stevens.

29th US Infantry Division badge.

Panic and confusion were rife. Both organisation and cohesion weakened, even before the infantrymen could fire a single bullet. Many soldiers, in a state of shock, remained on the sand, sitting or lying down. The most valiant among them took a deep breath and tried to group together. Units were scattered over hundreds of metres. The officers that were still alive struggled to maintain a semblance of organisation amidst the chaos. In less than 15 minutes, the company had been torn to shreds. Of its 200 men, three quarters had been killed or wounded. With the exception of Lieutenants Elijah Nance and Edward Gearing, all of the company's officers were dead or seriously wounded. The small village of Bedford in Virginia lost 21 of its inhabitants during this one ill-fated day.

The 116th RCT's Company B, which made a scattered landing in the Dog Green sector, fell directly under fire from *WN 72*. Once more, it was absolute carnage. The men were slain inside their barges. Captain Ettore Zappacosta, in command of the unit, was fatally wounded.

The 2nd Rangers' Company C landed at H+15 at the western extremity of Vierville beach, entrusted with the mission of walking to Pointe de la Percée. Barely had it grounded, when Captain Ralph E. Goranson's LCA418 was hit 4 times and split in two. A dozen men were killed by the blast. A German gunner shot down fifteen men as they tried to leave LCA1038. Of a total of 64 men, 33 were already dead or wounded. The Germans threw stick grenades to try to dislodge the Rangers who had managed to make it to the foot of the cliff. The weakened company could not use the solidly defended D-1 exit. Goranson consequently sent a reconnaissance troop westwards. Lieutenant Moody found a feasible escarpment 300 metres away. The Rangers climbed the rock face using their Toggle ropes and their bayonets. After clearing the area round a damaged stone house, built in the hollow of the cliff, they infiltrated the maze of trenches and tried to reduce *WN 73* to silence. They were helped by elements from the 116th RCT's Company B, whose LCM had grounded at the foot of the position.

D-1 exit (Vierville)

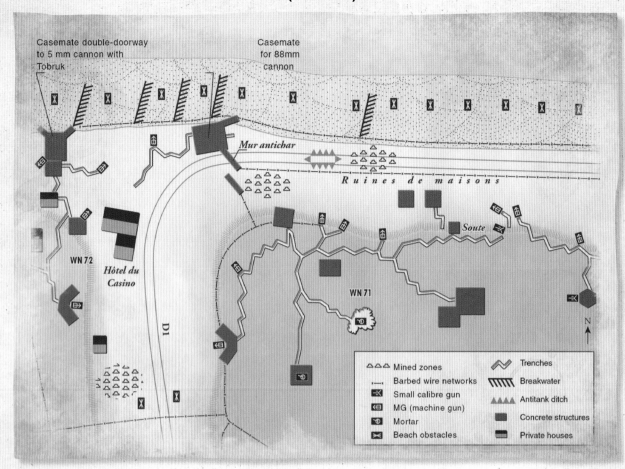

Casemate double-doorway to 5 mm cannon with Tobruk

Casemate for 88mm cannon

Mur antichar

Ruines de maisons

WN 72

Hôtel du Casino

D1

Soute

WN 71

N

△△△ Mined zones		〰 Trenches
╷╷╷ Barbed wire networks		╫╫╫ Breakwater
⊠ Small calibre gun		▲▲▲ Antitank ditch
⊡ MG (machine gun)		▮ Concrete structures
⬗ Mortar		▭ Private houses
⋈ Beach obstacles		

5th Rangers M1 helmet.
© P. Caje Collection

Toggle Rope used by the Rangers to climb up the cliff.
© VD Collection

EASY RED

The situation was equally dramatic for the units landed further east. The 16th RCT was in charge of clearing the E-1 exit before climbing up to the heights and bypassing Colleville before heading for Mont Cauvin, 5km away. Companies E and F landed at 6.37am on Easy Red. The LCVPs drifted with the current, to ground on an 800 metre front directly opposite *WN 61* and *WN 62*. Part of the 116th RCT's Company E was among them.

This LCVP from *USS Samuel Chase* has been hit on its way to the beach. Dalba L. Nivens, a helmsman, is landing his Team Assault Company and successfully putting out the fire along with a mechanic. © NARA

The men immediately fell victim to German mortar and machine gunfire. The first were cut in two by the bursts. The gunners concentrated their fire on the ramps, mowing down the American soldiers. Survivors tried to work their way along the sides of the ramps or to stride across the flanks to jump into the water. They were surprised to find themselves 400 metres from the shoreline with water up to their shoulders. They struggled not to drown. Terrified by the intensity of enemy fire, the barge pilots preferred to ground on the first sand banks rather than to continue straight ahead, driven by the waves. The infantrymen fell into invisible channels shaped by the tide. They offloaded their equipment and heavy weapons. The liquid mass did not protect their bodies from the projectiles. The men threw themselves to the ground behind the beach obstacles. The enemy gunners aimed at the antitank mines that surmounted the obstacles, behind which groups of GIs were crouched.

TESTIMONY

"I stopped in the water and pressed myself against a tetrahedron with two soldiers crouching to my right. Bullets ricocheted all around, without reaching me, when the two guys collapsed on the sand: hit! Their bodies in the waves. The place was not very safe. I decided to crawl to the left with my section. We had to climb over the bodies, bypass the smoking tank carcasses, clear the scattered equipment. I lay down under the shelter of a tetrahedron, under machine gunfire. Ten minutes later, I could feel someone tugging at my foot. It was one of my men waking me up unawares. The four Dramamine tablets I had taken on the boat had made me sleep in the midst of the skirmish."

First Lieutenant Karl Wolf, 16th Infantry Regiment, Company F

H-Hour on the Easy Red sector.
© NARA

Once on the sand, those who had survived the first assault wave were totally exhausted and incapable of retaliating. Despite measures taken to protect them from the sea water and the sand, the majority of radios and firearms were unfit for use. Many soldiers were in a state of shock, whilst others, more nonchalant, seemed oblivious to the dangers they faced. They were to cross over 200 metres of sand, without the slightest cover, before crouching under the stone embankment that lined the beach. Those who stopped in their tracks and tried to get themselves organised, to find shelter or simply to take a deep breath, were condemned to certain death. The soldiers crawled to avoid drawing the enemy's attention. Bullets and white-hot shrapnel caused terrible wounds. Dislocated and abandoned bodies and equipment were strewn across the sand or drifted on the waters. The skeletons of blazing barges and tanks completed the apocalyptic scene.

Four tanks covered the infantry with their guns and other weapons on board. The companies that landed opposite *WN 62* were wiped out. There were only 2 surviving officers from Company F and Company E suffered 105 lost or wounded soldiers. From one end of the beach to the other, German guns, mortars and machine guns continued to rake the sand. From their observation posts, the confident German officers incessantly forwarded new firing coordinates to the artillery batteries.

1st US Infantry Division insignia.
© VD Collection

16th infantry regiment crest
© VD Collection

TESTIMONY

"We suffered huge losses in less than fifteen minutes. I tried to count my men, lying all around me: only 13 of us were left, out of 188, not one single officer. The bullets ricocheted all around us, we did not have the slightest protection, the slightest shelter, apart from the useless enemy tetrahedrons installed on the beach or the bodies of our already dead buddies."

Captain Edward Wozenski, 1st US Infantry Division, 16th Regiment, Company E

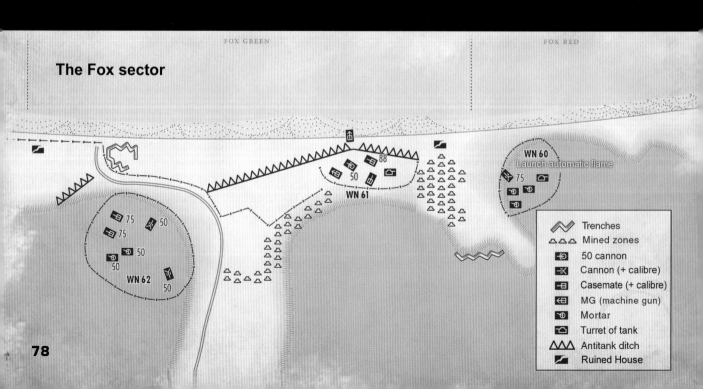

The Fox sector

FOX GREEN   FOX RED

WN 60
Launch automatic flame
75

WN 61
88
50

WN 62
75   50
75
50
50
50

	Trenches
	Mined zones
	50 cannon
	Cannon (+ calibre)
	Casemate (+ calibre)
	MG (machine gun)
	Mortar
	Turret of tank
	Antitank ditch
	Ruined House

THE BEAST OF OMAHA

Heinrich Severloh, who was aged just 21 years, spent over a year on the Eastern Front. After suffering from serious frostbite, he fell seriously ill and nearly died. He was sent to Normandy to convalesce. Posted to *Regiment 352*, he became the orderly of *Oberstleutnant* Bernhardt Frerking, in command of the *1. Batterie*, based in Houtteville.

On the morning of the 6th of June, the 2 men were with two corporals in the *WN 62* artillery observation bunker. They endured the bombardments and gradually watched the Allied armada emerge from the sea mist. Severloh plunged into his combat position, removed the hood of his machine gun, installed a cartridge belt and began to pray. He watched the barges as they grounded 400 metres from the shoreline.

Heinrich Severloh photographed in 1943.

Through his sight, Severloh could see the American infantrymen leaving the barges in single file and wading through the water with their rifles held above their heads. As the first among them prepared to leave the water, the Silesian firmly placed his hand on the stock of his MG42 and pressed the trigger. His first burst hit the sand. He raised the gun by an inch and launched a second burst, then followed the column as far as the barge, causing death and destruction.

It was a total surprise to the GIs, who were convinced that no German could have survived the tonnes of bombs and shells they had been subjected to. As the minutes went by, Severloh saw more and more men collapse under his incessant fire. He stopped counting them. As the tide gradually came in, the beach was transformed into an incredible shambles. It was strewn with the wrecks of vehicles, barges and chests. The dead bodies were swept in and out by the sea. Severloh, his eye pinned to the crosshair, the stock firmly wedged under his arm, continued mechanically. He launched short bursts to economise on ammunition. He only stopped long enough for the gun to cool, continuing his deadly deed by firing on isolated targets with a *Mauser* rifle.

M-42 *Heer* Drillich tunic.

Barrel of an MG-42 machine gun, a formidable weapon thanks to its rate of fire of 1,200 shots/minute. © Mémorial de Caen

Case of ammunition for an MG. © VD Collection

Early afternoon, the young Swabian was still at his position. Shellfire had transformed *WN62* into a lunar landscape. Its hollow had partly been filled by the earth stirred by explosions. Kneeling behind his gun, he observed, identified and fired almost unconsciously on the soldiers that were already cramped along the thalweg, and on those that continued to land. The men from the Big Red One were eager to neutralise this gunner who had killed and wounded so many of their fellow soldiers. Their fire gained in accuracy. The line drawn by Severloh's bullets betrayed his position. A bullet ripped off his machine gun foresight and wounded him in the face. The destroyer *USS Doyle* and the tanks were also now targeting him. The blow of a shell tore the weapon from his hands. The majority of the combat positions around him were empty. Frerking gave orders to cease fire at 3.30pm. The successfully infiltrated American soldiers laid into the runaways. Severloh and a non-commissioned officer managed to reach *WN63* in Saint-Laurent. All the others were killed, including Frerking. Severloh was taken prisoner that night, during the disengagement, and was sent to England then the United States. *"Heinrich Severloh estimated having fired 12,000 cartridges on the 6th of June."*

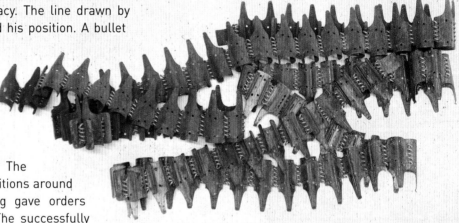

Fragment of an MG cartridge belt. © Mémorial de Caen

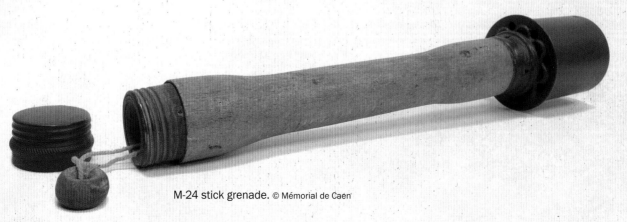

M-24 stick grenade. © Mémorial de Caen

2nd LIEUTENANT HILL'S HELMET

Kenneth W. Hill enlisted in July 1943 and left California as a simple infantryman. At the age of 30, he joined one of the US Army's most prestigious units: the Big Red One. He proved himself and was promoted to the grade of 2nd Lieutenant. On the 6th of June, as Intelligence & Reconnaissance Platoon Leader for the 16th RCT, Hill landed in the Easy Red sector at H+30. He left his LCVP and headed, with the other survivors from his Assault Team, towards the top of the beach to seek refuge behind a life-saving wall of pebbles. Automatic firearms and mortars raked the beach, bringing death. Hill was wounded in the right eye by shrapnel. He was shot in the thigh half an hour later. The officer was later evacuated to England. His regimental numbered helmet, now an orphan, was found several hours later by 2nd Lieutenant Downes from the 26th Infantry Division. The helmet's new owner used it as far as the Ardennes where he was, in turn, wounded.

Lieutenant Hill © Big Red One Museum

© Big Red One Museum

THE FALL OF *WN60*

The 16th Infantry Regiment's Company L landed at 7am at the eastern extremity of the Fox Green sector. One barge sunk in the sea; another was destroyed by the artillery immediately after grounding. Thirty-four men were shot down by machine guns as they ran towards the cliff under *WN 60*. The 6th Naval Beach Battalion established a temporary first-aid post. The unit, which still had 125 men, had managed to preserve its cohesion. Two sections, led by 2nd Lieutenant Cutler, headed towards exit F-1, a small dell at the end of which stood the Hamlet of Cabourg. Concurrently, the 4 LCAs that were transporting Company I and that had drifted towards Port-en-Bessin, followed the cliff line to ground at around 8am. One barge was

set on fire by an antitank gun. Informed of the situation, Kraiss ordered for a battalion to be sent to Colleville to launch a counter-attack between *WN 60* and *WN 62*.

The GIs climbed up the steep slope to come across the barbed wire that surrounded *WN 60*, simultaneously spurring German retaliation. Captain Armellino was seriously wounded as he tried to join 2 tanks from the 741st Tank Battalion, in order for them to support the assault. However, 1st Lieutenant Jimmy W. Monteith managed to reach them, under showers of bullets. He guided them through the mine field up to their firing positions. The tanks reduced several machine

War correspondent Ernest Taylor's photo report shows a group of infantrymen alongside the cliff immediately below the hamlet of Cabourg and *WN 60*. Most of these men are from the 16th RCT's 3rd Battalion. A first-aid post has been established at the foot of the cliff to treat wounded or shocked soldiers. © NARA

gun positions to silence and enabled the infantry to set foot on the plateau, after blowing up the barbed wire network that encircled the strong point. The destroyer *USS Doyle* covered their progression. The Americans sustained a violent counter-attack, finding themselves surrounded by German troops. Monteith was killed during his attempt to break through the enemy chain. He was decorated with the Medal of Honor for his bravery. The rest of Company L managed to bypass the German position, which finally fell at 9.30am. In the meantime, 2 patrols were sent towards Cabourg and Le Grand Hameau.

First aid dressing.

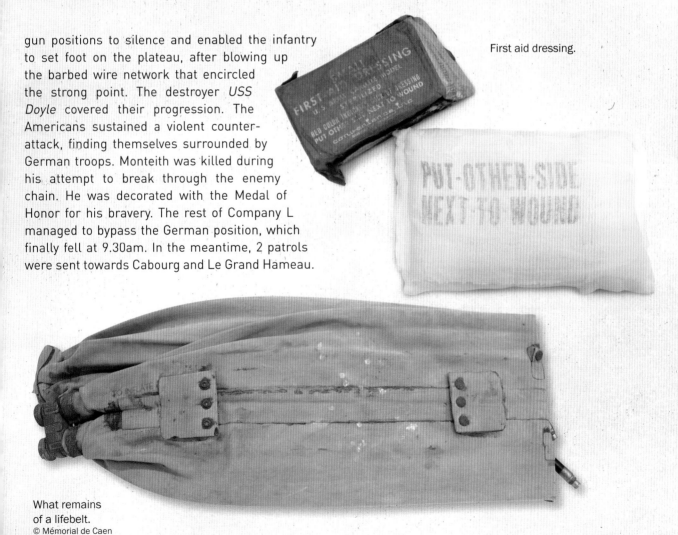

What remains of a lifebelt.
© Mémorial de Caen

THE MAGNIFICENT ELEVEN

The famous photo journalist Robert Capa, born Endre Friedmann, who covered the conflict on behalf of *Life Magazine*, had already taken part in operations in North Africa and Sicily with the illustrious Big Red One. On this occasion, he landed on Omaha with the first wave of assault.

At around 7.30am, Capa's LCVP hit the sand in the Easy Red sector, in the vicinity of exit E-3. He was accompanying a Team Assault Company from the 16th RCT's Company E. The men thrust forward under the gaze of the photographer who was to the rear of the barge. With his Contax camera in hand, Capa captured the scene before the crew master urged him to leave the barge by giving him a kick in the right place.

A narrow band of sand and an abrupt escarpment could be seen in the distance. Four Sherman tanks advanced slowly, followed by clusters of infantrymen. To protect themselves against enemy fire, some men lay flat on their stomachs in front of the steel tetrahedron. Others, stooping under the weight of their packs, struggled their way through the bullet-stabbed waters. The sound of the explosions and the staccato of firearms mingled with their screams. Out of breath, Capa sat with his back against an obstacle and took pictures of extraordinary intensity.

After half an hour, he decided to escape this hell, just half an hour after he'd landed there. He headed seawards, helping, on his way, a wounded soldier to board an LCI that then left the beach at 8.30am. He felt guilty for having panicked. Exhausted, he was transferred to a hospital ship that took him to England. Back in Weymouth, Capa entrusted his precious spools to a motorcyclist in charge of taking them quickly to the *Life* office in London for them to be developed. However, as he tried to process them quickly, the young

Rolleiflex 622 Old Standard camera – the same model as the one used by Robert Capa during his crossing. On the beach, he used a Contax II, which was more compact and faster to focus.
© VD Collection

Only 4 photographers were certified to land with the infantry on the beaches on the 6th of June and *Life* successfully placed 2 of them: Bob Landry on Utah and Robert Capa on Omaha; the 2 other photographs were Peter J. Carroll for *Associated Press (AP)* and Bert Brandt for *Acme Pictures*.

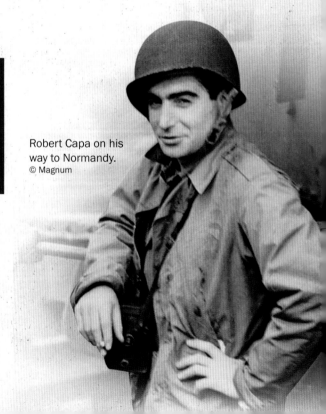

Robert Capa on his way to Normandy.
© Magnum

"The war correspondent has his stake – his life – in his own hands, and he can put it on this horse or on that horse, or he can put it back in his pocket at the very last minute. I am a gambler."

Robert Capa, Slightly Out of Focus, 1947.

"If you were going to photograph people dying, you had to share their danger."

Capa took to the sea and landed again on Omaha on the 8th of June to follow the American troops through the hedgerow hell, in Brittany and even as far as Germany. He was killed by a mine in Indochina an 1954.

photographic laboratory technician Dennys Banks accidentally destroyed most of the negatives. The only 11 pictures to be salvaged were sent to New York in time for the issue published on the 19th of June. They were used by many daily newspapers across the globe thanks to the Signal Corps' radiophoto department.

"My beautiful France was repugnant and horrible, [...] The men on my boat waded through water as tall as them, ready to shoot, the beach smoking behind them, all of this perfect for a photographer."

Robert Capa, *Slightly Out of Focus,* 1947.

Capa's pictures were published in *Life* Magazine's 19th June 1944 issue.

© Magnum

85

A makeshift grave in the form of a Ranger's helmet placed on what remains of a Vickers K Gun. The gun was recovered by the Rangers on one of the ladders that were mounted on DUKWs to increase their firing power. © NARA

CHAPTER 5

POINTE DU HOC

Eighty-five Douglas A-20 Havoc light bombers dropped a hundred tonnes of bombs on Pointe du Hoc to seal the battery's destruction. © NARA

THE APPROACH

The Rangers from Force A left *HMS Ben Machree* and *HMS Amsterdam* at around 4 in the morning. At 5.55am, the 305 and 355 mm guns aboard the

The site after naval and aerial bombing. © Mémorial de Caen

battleships *USS Arkansas* and *USS Texas*, cruising 17km off the coast, bombarded the battery for 30 minutes. The plateau was wiped out by 255 large calibre shells. Nineteen B-26 Marauder bombers belonging to the 391st Bomb Group finished the job 25 minutes later.

As the battle raged on Omaha, a short distance away, 12 LCAs and 4 DUKW amphibious trucks transporting the 2nd Rangers' Companies D, E and F made their way to Pointe du Hoc. The two columns were guided by the ML 104 Motor Launch and LCS 91 and 102.

The 20km that separated them from their targets seemed interminable. The Rangers were soaked to the skin and prone to sea sickness. Their transport vessels were flooded by high waves and tossed by the swell, heeling dangerously. LCA 914 sank just 15 minutes after its departure. LCA 860 overturned a little later. The castaways were recovered by the Coast Guards and evacuated to England.

Poor visibility and strong currents led the barges to drift towards Pointe de la Percée, some 3km to the east of Pointe du Hoc. Colonel Rudder, who was aboard LCA 668, realised their mistake and had their trajectory corrected. As they sailed parallel to the coast, the 2 columns became the target of the German defences posted at *WN 74*. A DUKW was hit by a 20mm gun and sank.

The first barge grounded on the pebbled shore at 7.11am, 40 minutes behind schedule, hence depriving the assailants of any element of surprise. The initial plan was to land on either side of the headland - Company D to the west and Companies E and F to the east. Company D had lost a third of its men following the sinking of 2 LCAs. Rudder consequently decided to launch the assault exclusively on the eastern flank of the headland.

Shrapnel from a 250kg AN M64 bomb. © Mémorial de Caen

POINTE DU HOC

The Germans had established *Stützpunkt 75* on the Pointe du Hoc headland. Work had begun in 1942 and was not yet complete early June 1944. The concrete gun emplacements housed six *K418 (F)* type *Cannons de 155 GPF (Grande Puissance Filloux)* guns belonging to the 2. *Kompanie, 1260. Heeres Küsten-Artillerie*, commanded by *Oberleutnant* Frido Ebeling. These open-air positions enabled guns to fire over 360°; however, the Germans decided to build casemates to protect them. As from November 1942, 500 French, Russian and Polish labourers were requisitioned by the Todt Organisation. A camp was established in Englesqueville-la-Percée.

A firing command post was built at the extremity of the promontory, looming 30 metres above sea level. The position was completed with personnel shelters, ammunition holds, DCA positions and Tobruks to house machine guns. Mine fields and barbed wire protected the position from an inland attack; however, the garrison had no antitank weapons. Only 2 of the 6 artillery casemates were completed. The battery was bombarded by the Allied aviation on the 25th of April and the 22nd of May 1944. One of the guns was destroyed.

The camouflaged firing command post at Pointe du Hoc. © NARA

A REGRETTABLE INCIDENT.

Shortly before *HMS Ben Machree* left Weymouth harbour, Major Lytle, who was to lead the 2nd Rangers into action, drank rather more than he should have, announcing to anyone willing to lend an ear that their mission was pure suicide. The Executive Officer was then taken to the infirmary, where he took a sketch out of his pocket showing that the Pointe du Hoc guns had been moved inland. The information had been provided by the Resistance and disclosed during an earlier briefing. Informed of the incident, Rudder left *USS Ancon* to board Lytle's ship, fearing that the news be divulged to the troops. A terrible fight broke out between Lytle, the medical staff and other officers. Captain Block, the battalion's doctor, was knocked out by Lytle, who was finally brought under control and dismissed from his command. Rudder decided to lead the mission despite General Huebner's attempts to dissuade him.

Grappling hook used by the Rangers to attach ropes.
© Omaha Beach Memorial Museum

ATTACKING THE WALL

The pebbled shoreline that runs alongside the cliff, the top of which is scattered with deep several metre-wide craters hollowed out by bombs and shells, prevented the DUKWs from establishing positions that would enable them to correctly deploy the ladders the Rangers had been provided with by the London Fire Brigade. The majority of attempts to throw grappling hooks from aboard LCAs proved ineffective for their ropes were soaked with sea water. Above them, the German soldiers had taken up their combat positions. They could see certain Rangers leaving their LCAs, laden with ladders and portable rocket launchers, whilst others were hard at work round the grappling hook launchers installed inside the barges.

The members of the German garrison who had survived the bombardments headed for the edge of the cliff. The Americans were subjected to intense light weapon fire coming from all directions, along with showers of hand grenades and mortar shells. A German machine gun, positioned to the left, targeted the foreshore and the cliff. Fifteen American soldiers collapsed before even reaching the foot of the cliff.

A group of Rangers in a defensive position on the edge of the cliff. A non-commissioned officer using a Cal .30 machine gun. © NARA

Rangers training in real-life conditions on the Isle of Wight.

Large calibre shells equipped with a delayed-action firing system were suspended from the cliffs on cables.

Nothing seemed to go according to plan, but none of this was enough to stop these hardened troops in their tracks. They furiously clung to the wet ropes. Many of them fell after just a few metres. The most intrepid among them set to climbing the damp rock face bare-handed, using their bayonets to attach sections of rope and ladder.

As they clung to the chalky rock, they could see the silhouettes of the Germans taking great risks on the edge of the cliff to find the best firing angle and to cut the ropes. The FM BAR gunners sent short bursts of fire in their direction to hinder their progression. Intervention by the destroyers forced the defenders to withdraw to their shelters. Hand-held mortars finally came into action and the grappling hooks eventually found secure positions amidst the networks of barbed wire running alongside the clifftop. Back on the beach, under constant gunfire, doctors and nurses provided first aid to the wounded pending their evacuation.

The Rangers' advance on Pointe du Hoc

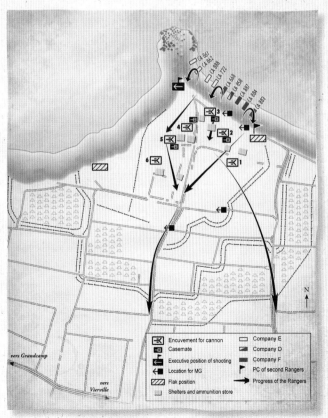

Map of Pointe du Hoc.

PRAISE THE LORD

To the east of the beach, a block of the cliff collapsed, forming a huge fifteen metre-wide gap. The nearby shelters had been abandoned. The Rangers climbed up the pile of rubble that had formed at the foot of the cliff, then scaled the last 10 metres that separated them from the summit, using ropes and ladders. Bill Vaughn, an excellent climber from Company D, was the first to set foot on the plateau at around 7.30am. He was quickly joined by his buddies. Small isolated groups advanced in successive waves amidst the craters and the fortifications that had been literally dislocated by the artillery and bombardments. They wormed their way through the trenches and the shelters. Skirmishes broke out here and there. Men fell, left, right and centre.

Rudder established his command post inside a crater adjacent to a deserted enemy DCA position. His signal officer could not communicate with the troops on Omaha, but he did manage to transmit an optical Morse code message to the ships out at sea, "Praise the Lord". The message meant that the operation was a success. The word "Tilt" would have meant failure. Unfortunately, his signal was

Colonel Rudder in front of a Morse code signal lamp.
© NARA

"The enemy captured the Pointe du Hoc strong point with two companies. From ships off shore, they fired special shells equipped with ladders onto the cliff, enabling them to climb the obstacle."

Report by the 3. Kompanie du GR. 726.

never received. The military staff on board *USS Ancon* believed that there was only one conclusion to draw from the absence of any message or lightning rocket: the 2nd Rangers Battalion had failed to scale the cliff and capture the position. They consequently decided to divert 8 reinforcement companies towards Vierville.

The Germans, who had successfully maintained several positions, fired on the assailants as they made their way towards the artillery casemates. A detachment commanded by Lieutenant Lapres tried to capture the firing command post. The radio antenna was destroyed; however, the grenades thrown and the bazookas fired by the Rangers were of no effect. The position held out till the following afternoon. The destroyers reduced several resistance nests to silence. Captain Masny attacked a Flak position located 300 metres to the south-west of the command post; however, firing was so intense that he had no choice but to withdraw, leaving fifteen men out in the field.

Sections of tube ladder used by the Rangers to scale the rock face.
© Omaha Beach Memorial Museum

LOOKING FOR THE GUNS

At around 9am, Sergeant Kershner Lommel and Staff Sergeant Jack Kuhn set off on a reconnaissance mission. They leapt across the road and headed for a hollow path. They found deep furrows, similar to those seen earlier behind the casemates. Suddenly, behind a hedge, they discovered five 155mm guns, meticulously lined up, their ammunition in piles beside them. Around a hundred metres away, the sergeants busied themselves around their artillery tractors. The two non-commissioned officers loaded thermite grenades into the breechblocks of the first two pieces. The resulting intense heat welded the mechanisms without provoking detonation. The sight devices were smashed using stocks. The soldiers recovered all the grenades their men had in stock in order to finish the job. A little later, Sergeant Frank Rupinski and a few Rangers from Company E blew up a large ammunition depot. Two couriers were sent to the rear to inform Colonel Rudder that the guns had been destroyed.

One of the five 155 GPF guns in firing position, destroyed by Lommel and Kuhn. © DR

The Rangers reached the casemates to discover, much to their astonishment, that they housed not a single gun. Wooden telephone poles had been installed to mislead Allied planes and any indiscreet observers. Only the wreck of an artillery piece destroyed by bombardments a few weeks earlier lay inside one of the gun emplacements. Vehicles had left deep furrows to the rear of the casemates. The firing command post was attacked using grenades and bazookas, but its occupants resisted a whole day before surrendering.

In the meantime, several detachments advanced towards the road that links Vierville and Grandcamp-Maisy, to establish a road block and to prevent the Germans from bringing in reinforcements. They set up their positions along the embankment that runs along the fields, parallel to the road.

Rudder sent Huebner the following message, *"Located Pointe du Hoc – Mission accomplished – need ammunition and reinforcement – many casualties."* The response came 2 hours later, *"No reinforcements available, all Rangers have landed (at Omaha)."* His men were to resist alone, pending the arrival of reinforcements freshly landed in Vierville.

Three Rangers resting inside a crater. The watertight bag on the rack, along with the telescopic antenna, suggest that this is a signal corps team. © NARA

USM1 carbine. © Mémorial de Caen

FORT ALAMO

The Rangers suffered three violent night-time attacks at Pointe du Hoc. Fierce fighting ensued, men firing at close range. Although inferior in numbers, the Americans pushed back the Germans, inflicting heavy losses in the process. However, the enemy continued to resist between the coast road and the command post established at Pointe du Hoc. The defensive perimeter was reduced to a hair's breadth. Late afternoon on the 7th of June, a tactical group from the 116th RCT and the 5th Rangers found itself at a standstill at Saint-Pierre-du Mont. Two barges brought Rudder's men a stock of ammunition and recovered the wounded and prisoners. Colonel Rudder, himself wounded, only had 90 men still fit to handle a firearm. They all awaited the ultimate attack, but were finally joined by troops from Omaha at around midday on the 8th of June.

Italian labourers and prisoners of war working for the Todt Organisation were captured on-site by the Rangers. © NARA

Heer cartridge belt and belt found in Englesqueville-la-Percée where the *9. Kompanie – 726. IR* was posted. © VD Collection

The wreck of a gun destroyed during the April bombings lying in its shattered emplacement.
© Mémorial de Caen

FALLEN FROM THE SKY

In this photograph, taken at Rudder's command post, he is standing beside a non-commissioned officer wearing a uniform with several pockets. On either side of his heavy helmet, we can see a white ace of spades and his sleeve badge represents a bald eagle. He is not a Ranger but an American paratrooper. The man in question is no other than Leonard Goodgal, a Screaming Eagle from the 101st Airborne Division, 506th Parachute Infantry Regiment, 1st Battalion. His plane had been hit by Flak and had crashed during the night. Four men had managed to escape the plane at the very last minute. Nils Christensen was taken prisoner on the plateau. Although wounded, Lieutenant Johnson had managed to reach the American lines. Leonard Goodgal and Raymond Crouch had, in turn, set foot on French soil at the foot of the cliff, not far from Pointe du Hoc, without realising exactly where they were. Early in the morning, they had watched the Rangers as they arrived on the shoreline and had progressed alongside the cliff to join them and take part in the combat.

British-made 101st Airborne Division insignia. © VD Collection

First on the left - Leonard Goodgal, easily recognisable thanks to his uniform.

Mauser rifle bullets found at Pointe du Hoc in the 1970s. © Private collection

Neutralising enemy resistance nests enabled
the American infantry to progress inland.
© Mémorial de Caen

CHAPTER 6

ADVANCING INLAND

HELL ON THE BEACH

At 7am, the second wave approached the shoreline. Four LCTs were put out of action before the Easy Red sector. LCT 540 was hit by 9 shells. The other vessels made a U-turn before even unloading all their tanks in order to escape certain destruction. The large Landing Craft Infantry (LCI) barges, laden with troops, arrived at high tide, cautiously making their way amidst the mined obstacles, now covered by the waves. The German gunners immediately took them as targets. Lieutenant Arend Vyn's LCI 91, which was transporting 200 men, was immobilised by a mine before being hit in the bow by a large-calibre shell. Sixty-three men were killed or wounded by the explosions and the resulting fire. LCIs 92 and 553 met with the same fate and had to be abandoned.

Seriously damaged, LCA 85 keeling dangerously.
© NARA

TESTIMONY

"Most of the guys were so sea sick that the only thing that kept them going was the idea of the combat that awaited them. Suddenly, we found ourselves in the middle of a minefield and the back left of the ramp exploded. One of my buddies, who was carrying a flamethrower on his back, was hit by a lost bullet fired by one of those Germans and exploded. Not only had we lost the right side of the landing ramp, but also many lives. It was the worst thing I had ever seen. The survivors had to jump into the English Channel and swim to the shore. You needed to remember to quickly throw off your gear in order to keep afloat. Then, avoiding the bullets, we swam to the beach and we ran for our lives. When I sat down and placed my hands on the sand to rest a minute, I could see blood flowing between my fingers."

Corporal Ernest P. Douvette, 6th Engineer Special Brigade, 293th IASCO

The rising tide reduced the beach to a narrow strip. Troops rushed behind the pebbled embankment to shelter from enemy fire. © Mémorial de Caen

At 8.30am, Commander L.C. Leever from the 7th Naval Beach Battalion ordered that the arrival of barges be suspended pending clearance of the beach exits. Poor weather hindered the progression of artillery units, which met with a number of difficulties. An LCT transporting vehicles from the 58th Field Artillery Battalion (FAB) was hit by a shell under its waterline. The vessel keeled before completely capsizing, taking all its vehicles with it. In just a few minutes, the battalion lost 36 men, 5 howitzers and 4 half-tracks. The 11 remaining howitzers were taken to Saint-Laurent early in the afternoon.

The 111th FAB, scheduled to land at H+120 to support the 116th RCT, met with total disaster. Twelve DUKWs each transported a 105mm M7 Howitzer, 14 soldiers and 50 shells. Laden by their cargo, 8 amphibious trucks went under off shore and 3 others were sunk by the German artillery. The last howitzer and its gunners were transhipped at the last minute onto a Rhino Ferry, already laden with howitzers from the 7th FAB which had in turn lost 6 of its 12 pieces. The 16th RCT lost almost all its anti-aircraft pieces and its howitzers. Only the 62nd FAB managed to set up its self-propelled howitzers in firing positions. The last howitzers were taken to Fox Green in the evening.

Punctured flask having belonged to Private A. Lawyer from the 16th Infantry Regiment.
© Big Red One Museum

Regimental number plate and insignia belonging to Lusby Charles from the 111th FAB. After their DUKW sank with their howitzers, gunners fought like simple infantrymen pending the arrival of new artillery pieces. Lusby was awarded the Purple Heart and the Bronze Star.
© VD Collection

WITH THE MEDICS

The medics did their all. They progressed without cover and nursed on the sand. Many fell alongside the wounded. Medical equipment and medicine were cruelly lacking. The beach offered no shelter. The large red crosses on white backgrounds that adorned their helmets did not deter the bullets.

Medics and doctors ran the length and breadth of the beach in search of the wounded. They discovered mutilated bodies, scattered limbs. All that remained of certain soldiers was a few bloody strips of flesh or scraps of uniform. Many men had been hit in the head. Stomach wounds caused internal bleeding which often led to death. The medics did their best to treat and stabilise the wounded. They cleaned

An unconscious soldier being given a plasma transplant by a medical team.

wounds by covering them with sulfa powder, put bandages on and administered doses of morphine to soothe their buddies' pain.

Amidst the commotion, the chaplains comforted the wounded and accompanied the dying till their last breath, their faith helping to ease their minds and to chase away the fear that overwhelmed them. This wartime violence had shaken the psychological balance of many soldiers. Some would later manage to overcome these tragic events; others would remain scarred for life.

Makeshift medical stations were established along the pebbled thalweg. US Army and Navy doctors treated the wounded, one after another, endeavouring to stabilise the most serious cases. Once cleared of mines, the antitank ditches housed makeshift medical units. Infantrymen were

Medic's haversack and its contents.
© VD Collection

TESTIMONY

"In war, there are no heroes. There are just guys who are scared. Among them, there are remarkable people, like our regiment's chief surgeon, Charles Tegtmeyer. I saw him on the beach making his way through the wounded, choosing the ones he could save and those who were condemned to death. He pointed them out... 'Yes, no... that man will live, that man won't.' "

Samuel Fuller, 1st USID, 16th Infantry Regiment, Company E

A medic completing a wounded soldier's information sheet.

A MIRACULOUS SURVIVOR

Private Harold Baumgarten landed opposite Vierville with the 116th RCT's Company B. The back of this 19 year-old GI's blouson was adorned with the Star of David and the inscription "The Bronx, New York". He was heading towards the antitank wall that blocked exit D-1. A bullet pierced through the upper part of his helmet and another smashed his Garand rifle. His fellow soldier Robert Dittmar, who was a few feet away, was killed. Baumgarten could see his squad leader on his knees, rosary in hand, cut in two by a burst of machine gunfire. He was hit under the left eye by shrapnel. After reaching the promenade, he recovered an abandoned gun and was hit by more shrapnel as he tried to help another soldier. Baumgarten, loaded with morphine, responded to Cota's call and climbed up to the heights. A bullet pierced through his left foot. The small guy from the Bronx simply wiped his wound with sulfa powder and continued, limping. He was wounded once more in the face at nightfall and was taken back to Saint-Laurent by ambulance. On the morning of the 7th, as he was lying on a stretcher, Baumgarten was hit in the knee by another bullet. He was evacuated by sea in the afternoon and survived his wounds.

recruited to contribute towards the healthcare chain. They carried the wounded on stretchers, under constant gunfire, taking them back to the barges for evacuation towards England. The wait seemed interminable for the wounded.

The barges transferred them towards specialised ships anchored off shore. The LSIs and LSTs had been modified to accommodate 300 wounded soldiers and to take them back to England. The most serious cases were transferred to the 4 British hospital ships that shuttled between the American landing beaches and Southampton.

Out at sea, the US Coast Guards cutters sailed to and fro along the beach to recover castaways. All the sailors' helmets were adorned with a skull and crossbones. The crew of CG-16 kept a chart to which they added a chalk mark for each rescued man. CG-16 could be proud of having saved 126 soldiers. A total of 1,500 troops owed their lives to the Coast Guards.

Wounded soldiers evacuated aboard an LCVP. One of them is wearing a German helmet as a souvenir. © Magnum

RANGERS, LEAD THE WAY

GIs anxiously watching the beach as the battle rages. © NARA

Colonel Charles D. W. Canham, 116th Infantry Regiment

With no news of their fellow troops engaged on Pointe du Hoc, the 5th Rangers headed for Vierville. Sensing the chaos that reigned before Vierville, the battalion's commander, Lieutenant Colonel Max F. Schneider, decided to land in the Dog White sector. The Landing Craft Assault (LCA) barges meandered their way through the partly submerged obstacles to land at around 7.45am. The two companies crossed the beach, sustaining minor losses. The 2nd Rangers' Companies A and B were less fortunate and lost half their troops, i.e. 68 men for each company.

At 7.30am, LCVP 71 grounded in the Dog White sector with, on board, Brigadier General Norman D. Cota, Second-in-Command of the 29th US Infantry Division and part of the 116th RCT's forward HQ. The general could see the troops gathered at the top of the beach and decided to take control of the situation. Colonel Canham headed eastwards to join the 2nd Battalion.

The men from the 116th LCT and the 121st Engineer Combat Battalion found themselves intermingled with the Rangers over 300 metres of shoreline. Cota walked up and down the beach with his walking stick, encouraging them to move on and to open the way for other units. Officers from the 116th RCT took over from him. With his arm in a sling, Colonel Canham also ran the length and breadth of the beach, giving orders and urging the men to continue along the 150 metres that now separated them from the foot of the cliff.

General Norman Cota. © NARA

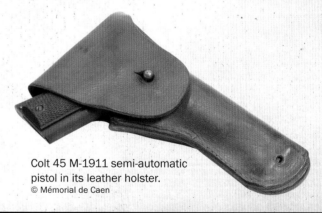

Colt 45 M-1911 semi-automatic pistol in its leather holster. © Mémorial de Caen

TESTIMONY

"I had exhausted an ammunition belt and I was waiting for Willi to load another one into the gun. He engaged the chain and I noticed that there were only 50 cartridges. Belts usually contain 200. I told him to charge more, otherwise it wouldn't last long. He simply replied that there were none left. I looked, but could barely believe my eyes as I realised that we were amidst piles of empty ammunition cases, belts and fired cartridges. All that remained of 15,000 shots!"

Private Wegner, 3. Kompanie, I./914. Infanterie Regiment, 352. ID

Under the impetus of their military chiefs, the troops crossed the parapet and set to destroying the double network of barbed wire that ran alongside the promenade. Several breaches were opened with Bangalore torpedoes. One by one, the squads ran across the marshy zone and began to climb up the steep slope via a narrow path.

The smoke that engulfed the abrupt slope was such that some soldiers put on their gas masks, in order not to suffocate. The 116th RCT's Company C reached the summit at around 8.15am, preceded by the Rangers. At around 9am, Company F advanced inland further east without encountering any major resistance.

Omaha Beach photographed mid morning. © Mémorial de Caen

Isolated elements from the 116th RCT progressed along the beach and followed suit. A Company B section successfully passed *WN 70* to later take control of the L'Ormel farm. The last groups left the beach at 8.30am. Cota's command group headed for the ridge where 600 men were now gathered. Machine gun nests and isolated gunners hindered the Americans' progression towards Vierville. Canham established his command post in the village around midday.

Shell fired by an 88mm gun. © VD Collection

LCI 83 reached the beach at 11 am when a shell hit one of its ramps killing several crew members. © NARA

TESTIMONY

"I jumped. The water was as high as my boots. On the beach [...] men were bleeding to death, crawling, lying all around; gunfire was coming from all directions. We plunged to take shelter behind anything bigger than a golf ball. Colonel Canham, Lieutenant Cooper and Sergeant Crawford were yelling at us to leave the beach. I turned round to say to Gino Ferrari, 'Let's get out of here!' Before I could finish my sentence, something hit me in the face. He had been hit in the head and his brains had splattered onto me. I kept going and the tide was coming in so fast that it covered him and swept him away. I couldn't see him anymore."

Private Felix Branham, 29th USID, 116th Regiment, Company K

Ernest Hemingway.

HEMINGWAY

The famous American journalist and writer Ernest Hemingway covered the event for Collier's magazine. He boarded Lieutenant Robert Anderson's LCVP which was headed towards the Fox sector. "Papa" Hemingway watched amusedly the grey seas covered with "bathtubs, gondolas and ships of all kinds". He observed the dark line drawn by the silhouettes of the warships. Blazing tongues licked out of the guns aboard the striking battlewagons *USS Arkansas* and *USS Texas*. The fearsome grumble of the heavy shells was like the noise a freight train might make on its way to heaven. The men saluted to the black clouds of earth and smoke that rose above the hills.

There were no control boats and the men had to fend for themselves. The naval officer was heading for the Dog White sector before finally veering towards the correct beach zone. Just like the ones before, the 7th assault wave fell victim to intense enemy fire. Six barges were destroyed by shells and mines. Hemingway observed the tragedy in the making. Lieutenant Anderson had just one thing in mind: to get away from this hell as quickly as possible. Once the infantrymen had landed, the barge immediately turned round and headed for the high seas. In Hemingway's article, published a few weeks later, he offered a detailed depiction of this tragedy and of the great confusion that reigned aboard his barge.

Hemingway and Capa photographed early August 1944.

"Just then one of the tanks flared up and started to burn with thick black smoke and yellow flame. Farther down the beach, another tank starting burning. Along the line of beaches, they were crouched like big yellow toads along the high water line. As I stood up, watching, two more started to burn. The first ones were pouring out gray smoke now, and the wind was blowing it flat along the beach. As I stood up, trying to see if there was anyone in beyond the high water line of tanks, one of the burning tanks blew up with a flash in the streaming gray smoke. On the beach on the left where there was no sheltering overhang or shingled bank, the first, second, third, fourth and fifth waves lay where they had fallen, looking like so many heavily laden bundles on the flat pebbly stretch between the sea and the first cover. I saw three tanks coming along the beach, barely moving. The Germans let them cross the open space where the valley opened onto the beach, and it was absolutely flat with a perfect field of fire. Then I saw a little fountain of water jut up, just over and beyond the lead tank. Then smoke broke out of the leading tank on the side away from us, and I saw two men dive out of the turret and land on their hands and knees on the stones of the beach. They were close enough so that I could see their faces, but no more men came out as the tank started to blaze up and burn fiercely."

Ernest Hemingway, war correspondent.

Admiral Kirk, Lieutenant General Bradley, Rear Admiral Struble and Major General Keen, *USS Augusta*. © NARA

AMIDST THE FOG OF WAR

Out at sea, aboard *USS Augusta*, Bradley received fragments of information on the indescribable chaos that reigned on the beach. Officers were sent on a patrol boat to get a clearer picture. However, their report left little room for optimism. The German coastal defences and artillery were intact and had crushed the first waves of assault and the Engineer teams had apparently failed to totally accomplish their mission. The sand was strewn with vehicles and equipment. The beach seemed to be totally congested.

"Situation on the beach exits in the Easy, Fox and Dog sectors still critical at 11:00 hours. The *352. Infanterie Division* has been identified. The 115th RCT received orders to clear the plateau to the southwest of Easy Red at 11:31. The 16th and 116th RCT have landed; fighting is continuing on the beaches, where vehicles are gradually arriving. Reports indicate a few captured Germans on Easy Green."

Report forwarded to General Bradley at 11.45am.

LCIs laden with troops were a prime target for the German artillery. © NARA

Damage to radios prevented land-based troops from communicating with their commanders off shore.

dry land. Fragments of message were late to reach the V Corps.

Bradley joined *USS Ancon* late morning and was given reassuring news for the first time since the start of the operation. The arrival of the second wave of assault had offered a semblance of organisation. The beach exits were still fiercely defended; however, a few combat groups had managed to reach the plateau via narrow pathways running along the banks of the hillside. Several German positions were captured from the rear and squadrons were on their way to Colleville and Vierville. Reassured, the general cancelled any plans to re-embark.

At this point, the commander of the First US Army envisaged interrupting the operation and redirecting forces towards Utah Beach and Gold Beach, where the landing operations were running pretty much according to plan. But beforehand, he decided to set the artillery into action to try to break the deadlock. At 9.20am, the naval guns and the LCT (R) barges entered into action, forcing the Germans to huddle inside their shelters. The storm of steel only lasted 25 minutes, but this time, the Allies hit their targets. The trenches and combat positions were partly plugged and telephone lines were cut, hence isolating enemy positions.

Generals Huebner and Gerow kept a watch over operations from the upper deck of *USS Ancon*. They had no real control over the battle. Two amphibious DUKW trucks with radio equipment on board passed a few hundred metres from the shoreline and reported back on the situation on

Bradley cancelled his plans to re-embark and boarded a speed boat to head for USS Bayfield, Force U's flagship. © NARA

Insignia of the 1st US Army.

FLAGSHIP *USS ANCON*

The cruise liner *Ancon*, launched in 1938, was requisitioned by the US Navy in 1942. It was used to transport troops before being converted to serve as a command ship for amphibious operations. The ship was equipped with extensive anti-aircraft weaponry and a modern communication system. *USS Ancon* took part in landing operations in Sicily and Salerno before heading for Devonport on the 25th of November. The flagship, which was assigned to the 11th Amphibious Force, left Portland on the 5th of June. On board: Rear Admiral Hall, commander of Force O, Major General Gerow, commander in chief of the V US Army Corps, Major General Huebner, commander of the 1st US Infantry Division and Brigadier General Hoge, commander of the 1st ESB Group. The room formerly occupied by the radar operator was converted into a command centre. A map table stood in its centre, whilst two walls were covered with maps of the assault sector. On the 6th of June, *USS Ancon* coordinated operations between the naval forces and the assault troops. Once the command units had been transferred to dry land, the flagship's LCVPs were used to transport troops and material. *USS Ancon* then returned to England before heading back to the Pacific Ocean.

THE SPECIALISTS

The 5th and 6th Engineer Special Brigades (ESB), reuniting a multitude of specialists, landed on the morning of the 6th of June. Their mission was to clear the minefields and the beach exits and to regulate traffic flow to avoid jamming. Before they could accomplish it, they assisted the infantrymen over the initial assault. They then installed the necessary facilities to ensure that men, vehicles and material could be unloaded. They were supported by Naval Beach Battalions. Temporarily placed under US Army control, these sailors cleaned and marked out navigation channels. They coordinated maritime operations via permanent links with the ships that were anchored off shore. They unloaded all vessels and evacuated the wounded. They only left Omaha upon closure of the Gooseberry late November 1944 to head for the ports of Le Havre and Rouen.

ESB insignia.

An ESB team member clearing a minefield. © NARA

ESB US M1 helmet belonging to a member of the 5th or 6th ESB. Its owner has painted it with special mustard paint, which changes colour in the presence of poison gas. The amphibious troops' emblem, surmounted with a white semi-circle can easily be recognised.
© P. Caje Collection

The Americans used a variety of objects to produce makeshift signs. This jerrycan was used to designate the presence of the 5th ESB's command post on the beach.
© Omaha Beach Memorial Museum

ON THE GERMAN SIDE

From one end of the beach to the other, the German infantrymen and gunners wreaked havoc among the Allied ranks. The staff from the *352. Infanterie Division*, who were kept abreast of the battle via a telephone link, seemed confident early morning. *Oberstleutnant* Ziegelmann, Kraiss's intelligence officer, succeeded in establishing a communication link with the officer in charge of *WN 74*, who gave him an account of the situation on Omaha Beach. Kraiss, convinced he had driven back the assault on Omaha, sent his reserve units towards Gold Beach to do likewise with the British vanguard. The German units were wiped out.

Nevertheless, the German resistance gradually weakened. The American assault troops succeeded in breaking through the German defences. Several strong points stopped fighting or were on the verge of doing so. The artillery batteries, which had exhausted most of their ammunition, began to fire piece by piece to save shells.

The first Allied inland penetration forced Kraiss to round up any available forces in an attempt to contain the enemy and to launch a powerful counterattack, but it was too late.

"Along the low tide mark that stretches from Saint-Laurent to Vierville, the enemy tried to seek refuge behind the obstacles. A large number of vehicles – and around ten tanks – were burning on the beach. The demolition teams had stopped working. Barge landing had been interrupted. The vessels remained out at sea. Firing from our strong points and by the artillery had proved efficient and had inflicted heavy losses on the enemy. A great number of wounded and dead soldiers were strewn across the beach. Some of our strong points had ceased fire; they were no longer answering their telephones. A commando unit landed to the east of this strong point and attacked *WN 74* from the south; however, after being driven back and sustaining losses, it fled towards Gruchy."

Report submitted by *WN 74* to the *352. Infanterie Division's* command post

German field telephone and *Feldfu B* radio. Resistance nests were linked to the German command by means of telephones, radios and Morse code signal lamps. © VD Collection

Camouflaged M-1940 helmet from the *352. ID* found in Le Mesnil-Rouxelin (hill 108) to the north of Saint-Lô.
© VD Collection

Recordings of telephone conversations recovered by the Americans after the battle offer an ongoing summary of events seen from the German side.

8 h 46 : "To the north of Saint-Laurent, WN 65, 66, 67 and 70 have probably been captured by the enemy. In front of WN 68, powerful enemy formations have landed, coming from larger vessels, approximately 150 men."

9 h 05 : "WN 61, to the north-east of Colleville has fallen into enemy hands. WN 62 is no longer in action with just one machine gun intact. The enemy forces have made a forward thrust between WN 61 and 62 towards WN 63. New and increasingly large formations have been landed from around fifty boats off WN 62. The 1. and 4. Kompanie reserve troops are on their way to the sector [...]."

9 h 15 : "In front of WN 65, to the north-east of Saint-Laurent, sixty to seventy landing barges are currently landing troops. No report from Pointe du Hoc. The situation before Grandcamp has not changed. WN 65-68 and 70 are occupied by the enemy. New and extensive landings have been seen from WN 65 and 66."

11 h 10 : "Contrary to previous reports, WN 66 and 68, to the north of Saint-Laurent, are still firmly held. However, Pointe du Hoc has been reached by the enemy with the equivalent of two companies. Available reserve troops have been employed to rectify the situation. Observers have reported that the enemy is firing on the cliff with special shells containing rope ladders, with which one can easily scale the cliff. Units serving WN 71 and 73 have been weakened considerably; they have been reinforced by pioneer units."

11 h 14: "[…] The situation on the left wing is critical for the enemy has already reached the church in Colleville. WN 60 and 62 are managing to successfully defend their positions."

11 h 40: "The south-east exit at Colleville has been captured by the enemy. New tanks have been landed opposite WN 62. A great number of armoured vehicles are gathered in front of the antitank ditch."

11 h 55: "The enemy has occupied the south-west exist with the equivalent of one section. New tanks have been landed opposite WN 62."

12 h 25: "[…] Our troops in position at Pointe du Hoc are surrounded by 2 enemy companies. A counter-attack has been launched by elements from the III./726 GR [...]"

12 h 35: "Colleville has been reconquered. We are still in possession of WN 62 and 62b; 61 is still occupied by the enemy including a tank."

12 h 49: "WN 60, 62 and 62b are now in our hands; at WN 61 an enemy tanks is still in position."

REINFORCEMENTS

To the east, 3 companies from the 16th RCT succeeded in setting foot between *WN 62* and *64* with no major losses. Men from the 1st Battalion opened a breach in the barbed wire network. Colonel Taylor, who had sufficient forces to attempt a breakthrough, vehemently jostled his exhausted men and urged them to leave the damned beach.

Small groups of infantrymen infiltrated the embankments, breaking through the enemy defences in several places. As Company C walked towards Colleville, *WN 64* surrendered to Lieutenant John Spalding's section.

The 18th RCT's 2nd Battalion landed in the Easy Red sector at around 10am - 30 minutes behind schedule because of currents and congestion on the beach: 22 LCVPs, 2 LCIs and 4 LCTs. Twenty-six barges were lost due to obstacles and mines. The regiment sustained minor losses. The last remaining resistance nests were immediately cleared. The arrival of 12 LCI(L) barges transporting the 115th RCT amplified the phenomenon. This regiment had initially been scheduled to land in the evening or the following day; however, given the difficulties already encountered, the Allies decided to deploy the force earlier than planned. Consequently, three battalions landed in Le Ruquet late morning, since exit D-3 was still under enemy gunfire. The 18th RCT's 3rd Battalion arrived in the afternoon.

The opening of new breaches by elements from the 37th and 149th Engineer Combat Battalions

18th infantry
regiment crest
© VD Collection

"There are only two kinds of men on this beach. Those who are dead and those who are about to die. Now let's get the hell out of here."

Colonel Taylor, 16th RCT.

The 214th Military Police detachment landing opposite Le Ruquet. © Mémorial de Caen

enabled Captain Dawson's Company G to leave the beach and to join forces with advanced elements at around 8am. The American troops were stopped in their tracks by machine gunfire on the outskirts of the village of Colleville. They finally got the better of the German resistance after 2 hours of combat. The GIs took over the first houses and recaptured the church at around 1pm. The *726. IR 1. Kompanie* and the *II/915 GR* were quick to react by surrounding the American troops positioned in the centre and the south of the village. The situation facing Dawson and his men became critical – to be exacerbated by friendly fire, since they had no radio to inform of their presence in the zone. The guns aboard *USS Emmons* brought down the church spire mid afternoon and, early in the evening, *USS Harding* fired 135 shells on Colleville. The 26th RCT arrived at around 5pm as German shells continued to shower down on the beach.

On the evening of D-Day, the German army had lost the battle on Omaha Beach. The 1st and 29th US Infantry Divisions succeeded in establishing a 2.4km-deep bridgehead. Vierville was liberated; however, fighting continued in Saint-Laurent and in Colleville-sur-Mer. Gerhardt, Huebner and Gerow established their inland command post in the evening. Five infantry regiments had been landed, i.e. some 34,000 men. However the artillery, anti-aircraft and logistic units were not as yet fully operational. Due to the delays generated over the morning in order to reduce the German defences and to gain control of the valleys that offered access

Troops with minor wounds being evacuated aboard an LCVP. © USCG

Seriousy damaged, *LCI-553* could no longer turn back and was abandoned by its crew. © Mémorial de Caen

inland, Force B was only landed as from 4.30pm. Barely 100 tonnes of supplies, of a planned 2,400 tonnes, had effectively been set ashore.

A Rhino Ferry making its way through the obstacles and the wrecks towards the beach, still under enemy fire. © NARA

THE BEACH EXITS

Although the lack of radio links prevented any coordinated action on the American side, as the hours went by, the Allied command eventually gained increasing control of operations. Time was of the essence due to the rising tide, for the incessant flow of men and vehicles landed on the beaches led to congestion over what had become a very narrow strip of sand.

Under Cota's impetus, sappers from the 121st Engineer Combat Battalion succeeded in blowing up the antitank wall that blocked exit D-1 below Vierville. The exit was opened early afternoon, yet it was far from safe. German gunners had returned to formerly abandoned positions and continued to make the American troops' lives a misery. The church spire in Vierville, believed to be used as an observation post by the Germans, was blown up by the destroyer *USS Harding* shortly after 2pm. *WN 72*, still in action, was bombed by *USS Texas* and *USS McCook* before being attacked by land-based troops. The German garrison surrendered; however, it took a good few hours before Vierville was totally cleared.

Inspecting German trench networks on the heights above Omaha Beach. © NARA

The Easy Green sector was still in a precarious situation, yet two tanks from the 745th Tank Battalion managed to open a route inland at around 8pm. *WN 65*, also still in action, continued to control exit E-1 (Le Ruquet valley). Once more, the navy was to have the last word. The destroyer *USS Frankford* took up position 1 kilometre away and hit the bull's eye. Several 127mm shells penetrated inside the embrasure of the bunker that housed a 50mm antitank gun used to cover the beach exit. Gunfire from *USS McCook* forced the rest of the German garrison to surrender. The *Nebelwerfer*

The American advance on the evening of the 6th of June

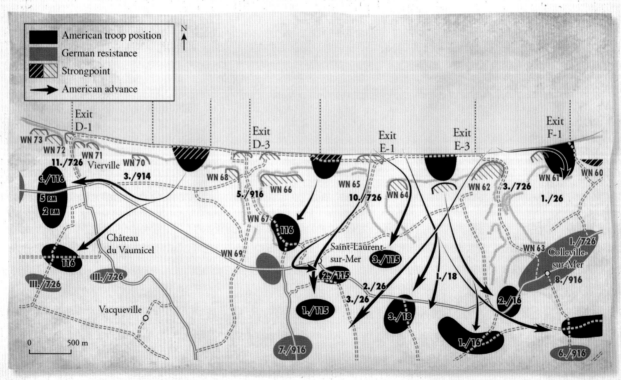

housed in *WN 67* were reduced to silence by *USS Carmick*. The last remaining resistance nests were immediately cleared.

Further east, demolition teams and ESBs managed to open two breaches in the pebbled thalweg, before clearing exit F-3. Supported by tanks and destroyers, the men from the Big Red One succeeded in muzzling the last German strong point defending exit E-1. The LCTs then rushed to the Fox Green sector near exit E-3, rapidly followed by Landing Ships.

This Marder III tank from the *352. ID* antitank unit has been destroyed inland. © NARA

Mid morning, this Sherman tank was equipped with its deep wading system. © Rights reserved

The German army used artillery pieces made in several different countries. This one is a French 47mm *PaK 181(f)* antitank gun – 1937 model. © NARA

The Le Ruquet bunker flag
© Omaha Beach Memorial Museum

THE LE RUQUET FLAG

Sergeant Dalmain H. Estes landed on the morning of the 6th of June. His units, vehicles from the 467th Anti-Aircraft Automatic Weapon Battalion, fell under enemy gunfire from *WN 65*, sustaining heavy losses. Several half-tracks were hit, forcing the men to continue on foot. Estes' radio operator's legs were blown off and the nurse was annihilated by a shell. The 50mm Pak gun at Le Ruquet prevented any movement until it was neutralised by the navy.

Accompanied by Private James Shelton, the non-commissioned officer entered the bunker and seized a swastika flag which he slipped inside his blouson. He religiously kept his trophy for fifty years before donating it to the village of Saint-Laurent-sur-Mer in 1994.

Inside the casemate.

The Le Ruquet bunker flag.
© Omaha Beach Memorial Musuem

AN ARTIST AT WAR

Manuel Bromberg won the famous George Bellows prize and studied at the Colorado Springs Fine Arts Center from 1932 to 1940. He was one of the 18 American painters selected in 1943 to accompany the American armies across the globe. Bromberg, at the time aged 26, was initially to be posted in South-East Asia, but was finally sent to England. During his stay in London, he inaugurated an exhibition of his works in Westminster Abbey, in the presence of Queen Elizabeth the Queen Mother.

As a Technical Sergeant, Brombert was scheduled to land in Normandy at H+20; however, Sir Kenneth Clark, the chairman of the War Artists' Advisory Committee, convinced his superiors to delay his posting to the front. He finally landed on Omaha Beach on the 9th of June 1944, taking with him a small spiral notebook and a Leica camera. The beach bore the scars of the terrible battle that had taken place there 3 days earlier.

He did a few sketches of the landscapes and the protagonists of this war, with attention to detail well worthy of his great talent. After the Normandy campaign, the American artist met with Picasso, Cocteau and Braque before completing his service in Germany.

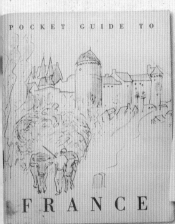

Pocket Guide to France.

Transhipment.© Mémorial de Caen

Burying the dead. © Mémorial de Caen

"It was an atrocious sight. Bodies were still floating amidst the waters. It was a combination of Dante's inferno and the greatest rubbish tip ever seen."

Heading inland. © Mémorial de Caen

Samuel Bromberg.

115

The body of this American solider has been washed ashore at the foot of an obstacle. Two Garand rifles form a cross to indicate the presence of his body.

CHAPTER 7

AFTER THE BATTLE

THE FIGURES

On the evening of D-Day, German losses were in the region of 1,200 men: 200 killed, 500 wounded and 500 missing. The number of prisoners is unsure. Losses inflicted on the American troops were of no comparison to those sustained by Allied forces on the other beaches. They represented 30% of the total Allied losses reported on D-Day.

For a long time, the number of losses varied from 3,000 to 4,000. The American historian J. Balkoski, is behind the most reliable study for it comprises not only the 2 infantry divisions, but also all other units associated in the operation. Human losses totalled 4,720 killed, wounded or missing. Equipment losses were also great, with 50 tanks and 26 artillery pieces destroyed. There is no figure for other types of vehicle; however, photographs taken after the battle bear witness to the destruction of a great number of trucks, jeeps and half-tracks. For the Navy, fifty barges and 10 larger tonnage ships were destroyed or seriously damaged.

A Coast Guards seaman standing next to an 88mm gun at *WN 61*, removed from its casemate. © NARA

German prisoners were grouped together on the beach before being evacuated. © Mémorial de Caen

Indian Head Division insignia
© VD Collection

The 2nd US Infantry Division landed on Omaha Beach from the 7th to the 9th of June. © NARA

American losses on Omaha Beach on 6th June 1944

US Army	Losses: 4,186
1st USID	1,346
29th USID	1,272
2nd & 5th Rangers	311
741st & 743rd Tank Battalions	175
9th Engineers Battalion	621
5th & 6th ESB	250
Autres	211
US Navy & Royal Navy	**Losses: 524**
NCDU	71
Naval Beach Battalions	128
Barge crews	310
Others	15
US Air Force	**Losses: 10**
Bomber crews	10
Total	**4,720**

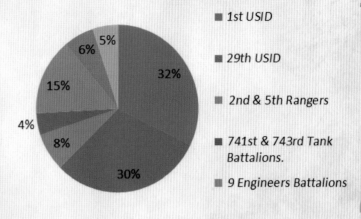

- ■ 1st USID
- ■ 29th USID
- ■ 2nd & 5th Rangers
- ■ 741st & 743rd Tank Battalions.
- ■ 9 Engineers Battalions

Source: Joseph Balkoski, Omaha Beach: D-Day, June 6, 1944. Stackpole Books 2006.

*Killed, wounded or missing

A GI standing in front of a dead soldier's body. © NARA

This Engineer unit soldier has just unearthed a terrible bouncing mine. © NARA

LSTs on Omaha Beach. © NARA

THE PORT ON OMAHA BEACH

As from the 8th of June, a different battle began on Omaha: the battle of logistics. An emergency airfield was built on the plateau between Saint-Laurent-sur-Mer and Le Ruquet by the 834th Air Engineer Battalion. It was operational as from the 9th of June and was used to evacuate the wounded.

The beach was a genuine beehive. US Navy and Engineer teams worked non-stop to enable men and materials to be brought in. Bulldozers were used to enlarge beach exits and wire-mesh was placed on the ground to prevent vehicles from becoming blocked in the sand. Over the first days, cargoes were transhipped out at sea by DUKWs, barges and Rhino Ferries – large pontoons with a shallow draught that were driven by powerful outboard engines.

Installation of the Mulberry A artificial harbour opposite Vierville began on the 8th of June. Fifteen old war and cargo ships (blockships) were scuttled in

Rhino Ferry outboard motor.
© Omaha Beach Memorial Museum

Barge rudder wheel.
© Omaha Beach Memorial Museum

The Rhino Ferries and the Phoenix caissons at Mulberry A suffered greatly from the storm. © NARA

shallow waters 1km from the beach, in order to form a breakwater and to enable navigation by smaller vessels and medium tonnage ships. The port itself was operational as from the 17th of June.

However, 2 days later, the weather took a sudden turn for the worse. Violent winds reaching force 6 to 7 on the Beaufort scale, together with 2 to 3 metre-high swell were to take their toll on the ships anchored inside the artificial harbour. Under the weight of the violent waves, the port elements began to drift, wrecking the Phoenix caissons and the nearby ships. When the storm finally came to an end on the 22nd of June, the outcome was disastrous. Port elements had been displaced, lost or destroyed. Twenty-seven out of 35 Phoenix caissons had been destroyed. Dozens of barges had been ripped from their mooring points and were grounded on the shore. The beach was but a heap of entangled metal carcasses. The US Army and Navy had lost considerable quantities of equipment. Engineers began to clear and repair without delay. The operation took over a week. The port elements fit for recovery were reused to repair and reinforce Mulberry B in Arromanches, which was later rebaptised Port Winston.

Overloaded trucks leaving a Rhino Ferry. © NARA

Seamen busy building the artificial harbour. © USN

Intense port activity was resumed. As early as the 23rd of June, LSTs set to unloading material and vehicles onto the beach. Seabees installed two floating causeways opposite Le Ruquet and Colleville, to enable barges to berth and unload directly onto dry land. New Phoenix caissons and blockships were installed to reinforce the breakwater. Twenty Rhino Ferry pontoons shuttled to and from the beach and cargo ships or LSTs in order to land vehicles. For their mooring manoeuvres, they were towed by bulldozers. DUKWs belonging to Amphibious Truck Companies were kept extremely busy, landing thousands of tonnes of supplies, ammunition and weapons. Supplies were then taken by truck to open-air depots located both near the beaches and inland.

Activity at the port on Omaha Beach decreased as from September, as the front drew further inland. It officially came to a halt on the 19th of November 1944. In total, the Americans successfully landed 500,000 men, 100,000 vehicles and around 1.3 tonnes of supplies on Omaha Beach.

Rhino Ferries

These low draught vessels were used to unload large ships anchored off shore. Driven by powerful outboard engines, they enabled ships to avoid long and painstaking grounding manoeuvres. These vessels were manned by Seabees. From the 6th of June to the 21st of October 1944, they transhipped some 94,495 vehicles and 422,195 tonnes of supplies towards Omaha Beach.

Seabees insignia. © VD Collection

DUKW

This amphibious truck, inspired by the GMC, was used for the first time in Sicily. Equipped with a hull and a propeller, it could quickly take men and material from transport ships to the front lines. On the 6th of June, DUKWs were used to support the Rangers on Pointe du Hoc and on Omaha to help transport howitzers. The Amphibious Truck Companies' DUKWs played an essential role in supplying American troops.

A Rhino Ferry transporting a DUKW and a bulldozer. Its powerful outboard motors can be seen in the foreground. © NARA

Landing Ship Tank (LST)

These flat-bottomed ships were 118 metres long and weighed in at 5,400 tonnes at full load. They were designed to ground directly on the beaches. They were equipped with hinged doors at the bow and with two decks. Their size and their autonomy enabled them to make oceanic crossings. They could transport 20 tanks or their equivalent in other types of vehicle or troops. Ironically nicknamed Large Slow Targets, LSTs were equipped with anti-aircraft guns and davits enabling them to house LCVPs.

A Whale platform offers shelter to Navy and Seabee teams. © USN

Wooden sign indicating the military cemetery. © Big Red One Museum

THE NECROPOLIS

The day after the battle, the 606th and 607th Quartermaster Graves Registration Companies began to gather together the bodies that were on the beaches and in the surrounding area. The American Supply Corps had planned to establish a cemetery on the plateau; however, the area had not yet been cleared of mines and a temporary cemetery was finally set up on the Dog White sector between Vierville and Saint-Laurent. German prisoners acted as temporary gravediggers to prepare the 457 tombs. German soldiers, British naval troops and men from the RAF were buried alongside the American troops. Each grave was marked by means of a simple wooden stake planted in the sand and the bodies were swathed in blankets.

For hygiene reasons and in order not to dishearten the incessant inward flow of new troops, the bodies were removed and transferred 10 days later to cemetery

Private Alfonton Ortega painting white crosses for the cemetery. © NARA

n°2, located near exit E-1 between Le Ruquet and Colleville. Within 10 days, 975 bodies, including 200 German soldiers, were moved and reburied.

Chest having belonged to Chaplain Fred E. Andrews from the 1st US Infantry Division. © Big Red One Museum

On the 12th of June, a solemn church service was given by the Chaplain Paul J. McGovern near cemetery n°1. © NARA

In May 1945, the American government decided to establish permanent national necropolises for soldiers killed on foreign fronts. Families were asked if they would like to repatriate their lost family members of whether they preferred for them to be buried in a military cemetery. The temporary cemetery in Saint-Laurent, where 3,797 American soldiers were laid to rest, was closed on the 14th of September 1947. The remains of German soldiers were transferred to the La Cambe German War Cemetery. Those who had been buried in temporary cemeteries were disinterred. Around half were returned to the United States. The others were transferred to a morgue pending their permanent burial in Colleville-sur-Mer.

The national necropolis in Colleville was inaugurated on the 18th of July 1956 on the plateau that overlooks Omaha Beach. Inside a semi circle, formed by the memorial colonnade, stands a 7 metre-high bronze statue by Donald De Lue which faces the square graves of some 9,387 American soldiers, sailors and airmen of all confessions. This monumental work symbolises "The Spirit of American Youth Rising from the Waves". A long semi-circular wall bears the names of the 1,557 soldiers whose bodies were never found.

Cardboard stencils used to inscribe the names of soldiers killed in action on temporary crosses.
© Omaha Beach Memorial Museum

View of the necropolis shortly after its creation from the Memorial that houses the statue entitled "Spirit of American Youth Rising from the Waves".

BRIEF BIBLIOGRAPHY

BALKOSKI Joseph, *Omaha Beach, 6 juin 1944. Le débarquement de Normandie.* Histoire & Collections, 2014.
BAUMGARTEN Harold Dr., *Eyewitness on Omaha Beach: A story about D-Day, June. 6, 1944*, Halrit Publishing Company, 2000.
DEPARTMENT OF THE ARMY, *Historical Division*, Pozit Press, 1994.
GAWNE Jonathan, *Jour J à l'aube Les troupes américaines en Normandie*, Histoire & Collections, 2012.
GOCQUEL Franz, *La porte de l'enfer*, Hirle, 2004.
KILVERT-JONES Tim, *Omaha Beach: V Corps Battle for the beachhead*, Combined publishing, 1999.
LEWIS Adrian R, *Omaha Beach: a flawed victory*, Gloucestershire: Tempus, 2004.
PRIME Christophe, *Omaha Beach: 6 juin 1944*, Tallandier, 2011.
MARI Laurent, *Omaha Beach: 1944-1994...GO!*, Saint-Laurent-sur-mer: L. Mari, 1994.
SEVERLOH Hein, *WN 62: mémoires à Omaha Beach, Normandie, 6 juin 1944*, Heimdal, 2004.
ZALOGA Steven J, *D-Day 1944: Omaha Beach, Osprey Publishing*, 2003.
ZIEGELMANN Fritz, *Die Geschichte der 352. Infanterie-Division*, MS B-741, 1948.

INTERNET RESOURCES

www.6juin.omaha.free.fr
www.omahabeach.mulberry.free.fr
www.history.army.mil
www.archives.gov

ACKNOWLEDGEMENTS

The author and Editions OREP would like to thank the collectors and the museums who have contributed towards the production of this book: Xavier Aiolfi and Émilie Weyl (Aiolfi & Partners), Marie-Claude Berthelot (Mémorial de Caen), Philippe Cage, Pierre-Louis Gosselin (Big Red One Museum - Colleville-sur-Mer), Copp Heroes Memorial Fund, Frederick Jeanne and Nicolas Leloup (Overlord Museum - Colleville-sur-Mer), Jean-Luc Cayez, Frédéric Normand, Florian Potin and Daniel Tréfeu (Omaha Beach Memorial Museum - Saint-Laurent-sur-Mer)

OREP
EDITIONS

Zone Tertiaire de NONANT - 14400 BAYEUX
Tél.: 02 31 51 81 31 - Fax: 02 31 51 81 32
E-mail: info@orepeditions.com - **Website:** www.orepeditions.com
Editor: Grégory Pique - **Editorial Coordination:** Kévin Decrouy
Graphics - Layout: Laurent Sand - **Design: OREP éditions**
English translation: Heather Inglis